I0796631

This book is presented to:

From:

On this date:

For Lydia and Everett,
May your hearts be filled with both the
longing of Advent and the joy of Christmas.

—Taylor

For Phoebe Elaine, "bright shining light,"
We pray you always know the radiant love
of the true Light of the world.

—Aedan and Natalie

Published by B&H Publishing Group, Brentwood, Tennessee

979-8-3845-1488-6
Dewey Decimal Classification: C242.33
Subject Heading: ADVENT \ CHRISTMAS \ JESUS CHRIST—NATIVITY

Manufactured in Dongguan, Guangdong, China by R. R. Donnelley, March 2025
1 2 3 4 5 6 7 • 29 28 27 26 25

The One We're Waiting For

An Illustrated Advent Devotional for Families

Written by
Taylor Combs

Art by
Aedan and Natalie Peterson

Brentwood, Tennessee

Contents

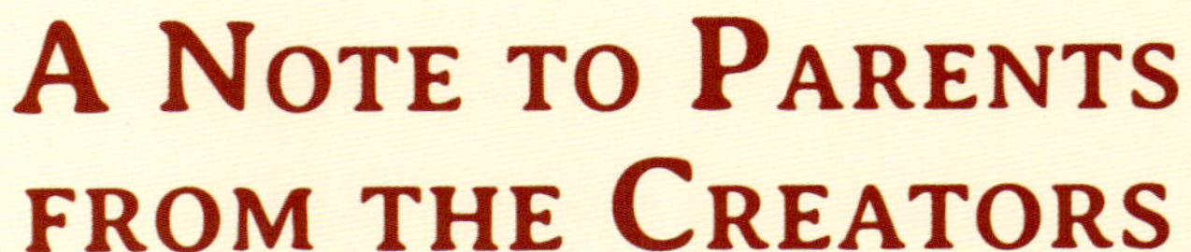

A Note to Parents from the Creators

In a 1947 essay called *On Fairy-Stories*, the author J. R. R. Tolkien coined the term *eucatastrophe*. It's a combination of the Greek prefix *eu-* which means "good," and *catastrophe*, an immediate and unexpected disaster. Tolkien's term refers to a sudden and unexpected turn of events that prevents an impending disaster. A clear illustration occurs at the end of *The Lord of the Rings* trilogy (I won't spoil the plot for you if you haven't read the books).

Tolkien, a Christian, referred to the birth of Christ as the *eucatastrophe of human history*. At the moment when things were darkest, when all was bleak because of human sin and brokenness and our inability to do anything about it, "the time came to completion, God sent his Son" into the world as a human being to redeem human beings (Galatians 4:4).

I, admittedly, have a bit of a melancholy personality. And I think that's in part why I love Advent. Advent is the perfect mixture of melancholy and joy. It's a raw, honest season of saying out loud the truth about the world's darkness—and yet, during this time, we dare to hope for *eucatastrophe*. And year after year, we find it in Christ. I pray this book will help you and your family share in the same hope.

—Taylor

We've found that our biblical imaginations come alive most during the season of Advent. The change in church rhythm, the special postures taken, the anticipation of a specific moment in time—all prepare our minds for a brighter picture of a cold night in a stable where the Creator of the world came as a baby.

Growing up, my (Aedan's) parents worked hard to assist that imagination. One of the ways was reading an Advent devotional every day of December leading up to Christmas. We turned off the lights in our house, lit candles, sang carols, and watched the puzzle pieces of the Nativity story gradually fall into place. Those moments shaped me deeply, and so I am incredibly thankful to work on a book like this.

Together, we hope that this book creates just a little more wonder, brings the Story just a little more into focus, and brightens the darkness a tiny bit more, until the One we're waiting for comes again.

—Aedan and Natalie

What Is Advent?

All people, at some point or another, walk through dark times. In fact, as I write these words, my own family has been through one of its darkest seasons, with the untimely death of a beloved family member. Perhaps you've experienced the same grief. Or maybe your dark time looked different—a crippling diagnosis, a prodigal son or daughter, financial hardship, the loss of health or strength, rejection by one you loved, or betrayal by someone you trusted.

Whatever the details of any particular difficult season, darkness often presents in the same ways. It leaves you disoriented. You don't know up from down, right from wrong, and you certainly don't know which way to walk next.

It's scary. You don't know what might be lurking around the corner, what next awful thing might reach out and grab hold of you.

It's lonely. With darkness often comes silence. *Is there anybody out there?* we wonder, feeling abandoned, left to figure things out on our own.

God's people have walked through various seasons of darkness, but maybe none are more significant than the Exile. When God first called Abraham, He promised He would give Abraham abundant offspring. He would be their God, and they would be His people, and among other things, He would give them a land—their very own, special, holy land where they would worship God, and He would dwell with them.

God made good on this promise, but almost immediately after He brought them to the land, the people began to sin horribly against God. They completely forgot Him, turned their backs on Him, worshiped other gods, and committed awful injustices against one another. Things got so bad that God punished them by purging them from the land. They were exiled through the hand of other powerful nations.

During this time, God's people must have felt that they were in total darkness. Where was God? Had He abandoned them forever? Were they no longer His people? They must certainly have been disoriented, scared, and lonely. Yet in His mercy, God gave them promises—both before and during the Exile—that it would not be this way forever. He would have mercy on them. He would deliver them. He would save them.

One of the greatest of these promises came through the prophet Isaiah:

The people walking in darkness have seen a great light; a light has dawned on those living in the land of darkness. You have enlarged the nation and increased its joy. The people have rejoiced before you as they rejoice at harvest time and as they rejoice when dividing spoils. For you have shattered their oppressive yoke and the rod on their shoulders, the staff of their oppressor, just as you did on the day of Midian. For every trampling boot of battle and the bloodied garments of war will be burned as fuel for the fire. For a child will be born for us, a son will be given to us, and the government will be on his shoulders. He will be named Wonderful Counselor, Mighty God, Eternal Father, Prince of Peace. The dominion will be vast, and its prosperity will never end. He will reign on the throne of David and over his kingdom, to establish and sustain it with justice and righteousness from now on and forever. The zeal of the Lord of Armies will accomplish this.—Isaiah 9:2–7

God promised through Isaiah that He would deliver His people from their darkness. He would send a Child, and that Child would become their great rescuer. He would rule and reign with justice and righteousness forever and ever. The people would again walk in the light.

The Waiting

With promises like this in hand, the people began to wait. And wait. And wait.

And eventually, God freed them from exile and brought them home. But still, things just weren't the same. Their glory days were over. God's presence was no longer felt in the way it had been. His people were not prospering but continued to be subject to oppressive nations. And, worst of all, God eventually stopped talking to them. For four hundred years, the prophets were silenced, and there was no word from God. But the people kept waiting.

This is the posture we take up during Advent. **Advent—the season in the church calendar leading up to Christmas, beginning four Sundays prior to Christmas Day—is the time of waiting.** Its name comes from a Latin word that simply means "arrival." Advent is not the joyous celebration of all that is merry and bright; rather, it is a time of remembering the darkness and longingly looking for the arrival of the One who will shine into that darkness. It is a time of recognizing and admitting all that is wrong in this world, and of leaning in with longing for the appearance of the One who will make it right. It is a time of daring to hope, of daring to believe those great promises of God's Word: "From ancient times no one has heard, no one has listened to, no eye has seen any God except you who acts on behalf of the one who waits for him." (Isaiah 64:4)

Still Waiting

But, you may wonder, why do we need to rehearse this posture of waiting when the promised Child has already come? After all, Christmas *did* happen, Christ *has* come, and a light *has* shone on those who walk in the darkness. Jesus came saying, "I am the light of the world. Anyone who follows me will never walk in the darkness but will have the light of life" (John 8:12). Indeed, all this is true! Christ is the Child promised to his people, the One who rescued them, the King reigning forever on a throne of justice and righteousness! But the Bible tells us there is another coming of Christ—another arrival, another Advent.

We live in the time between the times. We live between the two Advents. Christ has come; *Christ will come again*. And until He does, much remains dark about this world. Much remains dark about our lives.

You feel it, don't you? Our world is still filled with the stench of death; we wait for the time when death will be no more, when it will be swallowed up by victory.

Our world is still filled with the presence and consequences of sin. Yes, Christ came to rescue us from our sins, and on the cross, He paid the penalty of sin for all who have faith in Him. Yet, we long to be freed from the very presence of sin.

Our world is still filled with injustice—with people mistreating one another, committing violence against one another, oppressing one another based on race or ethnicity, income or class, religion or political persuasion.

Yes, much is still dark in our world—and in our own hearts. And for this reason, *we are still waiting*. We are still waiting for the One. He has come, but He will come again, and when He does, He will make all things right.

How to Observe Advent

There is no command in the Bible that Christians *must* observe Advent. But of course, there's no command that we must celebrate Christmas Day or Easter either! Rather, this is something many Christians have found helpful to their lives and glorifying to God for many centuries. Since at least the fifth century, Christians have observed this waiting period, this preparation leading up to Christmas.

The four great themes of Advent are hope, peace, joy, and love, with each of the four weeks representing a theme. The four themes are also signified by candles in an Advent wreath: three purple candles, a pink candle (for the third week's theme, joy), and the Christ candle, a white candle in the middle of the wreath to be lit on Christmas Eve.

Perhaps your church already observes Advent and incorporates these elements. Either way, you may also want to incorporate them into your family's life during this season. Many families have found it helpful to include the wreath and candles into a family devotional time during Advent. You may also find it helpful to use a resource like the *Book of Common Prayer*, which includes "collects," or prayers, for each week of Advent.

We hope this book will be another resource you can utilize in your family's observation of Advent. *The One We're Waiting For* is all about looking, longing, and leaning into the Advent—the arrival—of the One who will make all things right, Jesus Christ Himself. You'll read more in the next section about how to use this book. Our prayer is that it will enrich your family's Advent season year after year, helping you make more room in your hearts for the Savior who has come and who will come again.

We Will Have Spring Again

In C. S. Lewis's beloved children's novel, *The Lion, the Witch, and the Wardrobe*, four children stumble through a magical wardrobe into a land called Narnia. They learn quickly that the land is under the spell of a wicked enchantress who has made it *always winter and never Christmas*. When Lewis includes this description, he's telling us that Narnia was stuck in a perpetual Advent. They were always *waiting*.

When the children find themselves in the home of a rather hospitable family of beavers—Mr. and Mrs. Beaver—they learn just who it is the Narnians are waiting for: the great lion, the son of the emperor from across the sea, *Aslan*. And, word is, Aslan is on the move.

As the Beavers share about Aslan, strange feelings come over the children—some feel brave, others feel lovely, and one shudders with terror. But they all know there is something special about this Aslan. Indeed, he is the one who will come and break the spell of the White Witch.

Mr. Beaver recites to the children an old poem about Aslan:

"Wrong will be right, when Aslan comes in sight,
At the sound of his roar, sorrows will be no more,
When he bares his teeth, winter meets its death,
And when he shakes his mane, we shall have spring again." [1]

This is the promise of Advent. This is the hope of Advent. There is One who has come, and who is coming, whose arrival is of infinitely more significance than that of a fictional lion in a fictional land called Narnia. Truly, when this One, Jesus, comes in sight again, wrong will be right, sorrows will flee in terror, the barrenness of our spiritual winter—the winter of sin and brokenness and death—will meet its own death, and we shall all have spring again.

We pray that as you and your family read this book, your minds and eyes and hearts will be drawn up to look in hope for the coming of spring—for the coming of the King.

[1] C.S. Lewis, *The Lion, the Witch, and the Wardrobe* (New York: HarperCollins, 1950), 79.

How to Use This Book

With the messages of consumerism everywhere throughout the holiday season, it can be difficult to point kids (and grown-ups) to the most important part of the days leading up to Christmas. But incorporating a daily Advent practice is a great way to celebrate the past and future coming of Christ amid holiday madness. Below are a few ways you can use this book to create a meaningful experience and tradition for your family this year and for years to come.

The Story

Each day, you and your family will begin by reading a story that points to "the One we're waiting for" and helps the entire family remember that the whole Bible points to Jesus. As you read the stories, keep your ears open for how the story reminds you of the One who's coming. A refrain is also included at the end of each story; consider saying that refrain as a family to remember the anticipation God's people must have felt as they waited for Jesus and to anticipate His return yourselves.

The Questions

To help everyone remember the story and consider how it applies to Advent and your lives, questions are included at the end of each day. Parents, you may consider reading ahead to decide if the questions are a good fit for your child or children's age ranges. For toddlers and preschoolers, you may only ask one question. For older kids, consider if you can age up the questions. Customize this part of the experience to your family and let it change year after year.

The Song

There is also a song in each devotion that you and your family can play and sing as you reflect. Enjoy your favorite version of each song on your preferred streaming platform or create a playlist to use every year. Each song is listed in order here.

December 1.	"All Creatures of Our God and King"
December 2.	"This Is My Father's World"
December 3.	"Great Is Thy Faithfulness"
December 4.	"Rock of Ages"
December 5.	"He Will Hold Me Fast"
December 6.	"O Love That Will Not Let Me Go"
December 7.	"How Deep the Father's Love"
December 8.	"Holy, Holy, Holy"
December 9.	"My Hope Is Built on Nothing Less"
December 10.	"Nothing but the Blood of Jesus"
December 11.	"On Jordan's Stormy Banks I Stand"
December 12.	"Lord, I Need You"
December 13.	"Anchor of Hope"
December 14.	"Before the Throne of God Above"
December 15.	"Once in Royal David's City"
December 16.	"Hail to the Lord's Anointed"
December 17.	"Come Behold the Wondrous Mystery"
December 18.	"In Christ Alone"
December 19.	"Come, Thou Fount of Every Blessing"
December 20.	"O Come, O Come, Emmanuel"
December 21.	"Come, Thou Long Expected Jesus"
December 22.	"Joyful, Joyful, We Adore Thee"
December 23.	"O Come, All Ye Faithful"
December 24.	"Silent Night, Holy Night"
December 25.	"Hark! The Herald Angels Sing"

The Ornament

If you haven't already, flip to the back of the book to see the beautifully illustrated ornaments that go with each day of reading. These ornaments can be cut out and hung with a simple string, or, if your family loves an Advent activity, they can be turned into keepsake ornaments per the instructions on page 176. After your family has finished the reading and the questions, hang the ornament as you listen to the song and consider what you learned on that particular day.

The Memories

You'll find several blank memory pages starting on page 170. Write down memories for each year you use the book. Maybe it's a funny answer to a serious question. Perhaps it's everyone signing their names to see how a child's handwriting changes over the years. You can even add a family photo with a little tape. These pages are yours to record whatever memories you'd like on them.

What If Advent Begins Before December 1?

Because Advent is organized around the four Sundays leading up to Christmas, only on rare occasions does Advent begin on December 1. If Advent begins before December 1, pick a few passages to read from the Bible, find a song to sing together, light your candles, and start preparing to introduce the tradition of this book on the first day of December. If Advent begins after December 1, you can still begin reading this book but wait to light the inaugural candle until the first day of Advent.

December 1

What Went Wrong and the One Who's Coming

From Genesis 1–3

There was a time in the very beginning when everything was good. Nothing to worry about. Nothing to fear. No hurt feelings. No tears.

God made the heavens and the earth, and everything He created was very good. But one thing was best: people. That's right. People like you and me were the most marvelous things God made.

The first two people were named Adam and Eve. God put them in a beautiful garden filled with delightful things, and every day, God came down to the garden to join them for an afternoon walk. God gave Adam and Eve a special job: they, along with all their sons and daughters, grandsons and granddaughters, were to work in and grow this garden until it covered every last inch of the earth, and they would all rule together as princes and princesses.

God knew what was best for Adam and Eve—He created them, after all. So He gave them a few rules. Now, you may think, *Rules? I thought you said everything was good!* But good rules are a good thing! God's rules would help Adam and Eve live the life they were made for and enjoy the world God made! The rules were straightforward: love God, love each other, take care of the earth and the animals, be fruitful and have children, and *don't eat the fruit from that one tree over there.*

One day, everything went horribly wrong.

A sneaky old snake strutted up to them and started talking. (Never trust a talking snake.) This snake asked them questions like, *Is God really good? Are you sure He's telling the truth? Does He really want what's best for you? Wouldn't it be better if you do what you want instead of obeying those silly rules? Maybe you should just reach out, take the fruit from that tree, and eat . . . .*

They listened. They took the fruit. They ate it. And everything fell apart.

The problem wasn't that Adam and Eve got hungry and needed a snack. No, the problem was that, at that moment, Adam and Eve stopped believing God was good—that He knew, loved, and wanted what was best for them. They thought they had to look out for themselves. And, well, people weren't made to do that!

At that moment, Adam and Eve trusted themselves more than they trusted God. The Bible calls this "sin." And this first sin broke everything: their relationships with the plants and the animals they were to care for, their relationships with one another, and all the people who would come after them. Worst of all, their relationship with God was broken. Adam and Eve had to leave the garden and go away from God's presence. Every person since—all their sons and daughters, grandsons and granddaughters, and you and me—has been born in this sad state away from God's presence. Born trusting—just like Adam and Eve—in ourselves more than we trust God.

Every person, that is, except one.

God created a good world. He created us for that good world—for unending life and unlimited love. When Adam and Eve disobeyed God, the goodness was lost. But there was hope. God promised them that someone would come and fix it all. He would obey God perfectly. He would trust God completely. He would never sin. He would bring people back to God and give us the unending life and unlimited love we were made for!

There is One coming, God promised. He's the One we're waiting for.

Song for family reflection:

"All Creatures of Our God and King"

Discuss these questions together

- *Why did Adam and Eve think they knew better than God? Do you sometimes think you know better than God?*
- *What do you think "unending life and unlimited love" means?*
- *God promised that someone would come who would fix everything. Who do you think that is?*

A Big Boat, a Giant Storm, and One Faithful Man

From Genesis 6–9

Adam and Eve had children, and their children had children, and their children had children. And things did not get better. In fact, they got a lot worse.

The world was filled with sin. No one trusted God. Everyone thought they knew better than Him. And the unending life and unlimited love God made the world for were a distant memory. Now, people knew only death, tears, and heartache.

There was one person—only one in the *whole world!*—who still trusted God. The Bible says he "found favor" in God's eyes, which means he knew that God loved him. His name was Noah, and he wasn't perfect. But he did trust God.

Noah's name means something like "He will bring us help." When Noah was born, his father may have said, "Maybe this one, Noah, will bring us help. *Maybe he is the one we're waiting for*."

God decided, because of all the evil in the world, to start over. He would undo the creation by sending a flood to cover the earth. Then, He would recreate the world using one set of parents from every animal—and one family of people: Noah's family.

God warned Noah ahead of time about the flood, and He told Noah to have faith and build a giant boat called an ark. God promised that Noah, his family, and the animals would be kept safe through the flood. When everything dried up, God would recreate the world through them.

Noah built and built and built. And after that, he built some more. Just in time, God sent all the animals to the ark, and He told Noah and his family to get in. Noah helped everyone get on board and scurried on to join them. Then, God Himself closed the door.

Finally, the rain came.

It fell for forty days without stopping. (Can you imagine a storm that lasts more than a month!?) But God kept the ark and everyone inside it safe.

When the rain stopped and the waters went away, Noah, his family, and all the animals came out of the ark. God promised, *I'll never send a flood like that again*, and then He gave Noah and his family the same rules He gave Adam and Eve: *live in the world and rule over it with love—love for Me, one another, and the creation. Be fruitful and have children, and you and your children will rule over the land as my princes and princesses.*

God kept Noah and his family safe through the flood and remade the world through him. *Was Noah the One?*

Sadly, as soon as things settled back down to normal, Noah failed, just like Adam and Eve. Noah stopped believing God was good and decided to do what he wanted instead of obeying God. Instead of using God's new creation to honor and praise God, Noah used it selfishly—just like Adam and Eve. Noah's son, Ham, made a bad situation worse by mocking his father, and Noah cursed him and his offspring. Things got worse and worse and worse.

Noah found favor with God, and God graciously used him to save his family from being destroyed by the flood. But just like the first people, Noah failed. The One we're waiting for will also find favor with God, but He will never fail. God used Noah to save his family from the flood, but the One we're waiting for will save us from the destruction we all deserve because of our sin.

There is One coming, God promised. He's the One we're waiting for.

Song for family reflection:

"This Is My Father's World"

Discuss these questions together

- *Before the flood, every heart was filled with evil all the time. What do you think it means to have a heart that is filled with evil?*
- *How do you think Noah felt when God told him about the flood?*
- *Noah failed and sinned just like Adam and Eve and just like all people do today. How have you sinned today?*

"I Love You, So I'm Going to Bless You"

From Genesis 12

God was still working out His plan to give His people unending life and unlimited love. Even though Adam and Eve broke God's rules after He placed them in a garden of delights, even though the world got so bad that only one person trusted God, and even though that one man failed to trust God in the end, God would not give up on His plans for His people.

One day, God called a man. (Not on the phone—they didn't have phones back then.) He just called the man's name out of the blue. *Abram, Abram!*

What would you do if God spoke to you out of nowhere? If you could hear His voice? What do you think He might say to you? Would you be nervous? Excited? So scared you'd just jump into bed and pull the covers over your head?

We don't know exactly how Abram felt when God started speaking to him, but we do know what God said. For one, God just started making promises left and right. *I'm going to bless you*, He said. *I'm going to make you famous, and you are going to be a blessing to the whole world. I'll be on your side—I'll be your God! Anyone who is mean to you will have Me to answer to. And I'm going to bless the whole world through you.*

God, it seemed, was going to bring people back to the unending life and unlimited love He made them for—*through Abram!* Maybe, just maybe, Abram was the One.

The other thing God told Abram was to get up and go—to leave his family, his home, his life, and go. Go where? *To the land that I will show you*, God said. In other words, *I'll tell you when you get there!*

Abram started off well. He showed amazing trust in God! He believed God wanted what was best for him, so he obeyed, left everything behind, and started going, going, going. But along the way, Abram made all kinds of mistakes. He stopped trusting God. He lied. He tricked people. And he disobeyed God directly. Why?

Because Abram didn't fully believe that God would bless him. He thought he had to get the blessing on his own—a mistake his children and his children's children would also make. He thought he had to *earn* unending life and unlimited love—but no person can earn that. God has to be the One to give it.

God didn't take back His promise when Abram failed. Amazingly, God doesn't work that way. We might expect God to say, *Abram, if you work really, really hard and do a great job, I'll bless you and be your God and take care of you.* But God just says, *Abram, I love you, so I'm going to bless you.*

Was Abram the One we're waiting for? No. God told Abram to leave his home and go to a new place with a promise of blessing for the whole world. But the One we're waiting for will leave an even better home to give His blessing to the whole world. Abram didn't trust God, so he tried to earn God's blessing by his own actions. But the One we're waiting for trusted God perfectly and earned God's blessing for the whole world.

There is One coming, God promised. He's the One we're waiting for.

Song for family reflection:

"Great Is Thy Faithfulness"

Discuss these questions together

- *Was there anything surprising about what God said to Abram? Why do you think God made all those promises to him?*
- *Would you be able to leave behind your whole life and go to a new place if God told you to? Why or why not?*
- *We learned that no person can earn unending life and unlimited love from God. Why do you think that is? What does that mean for us?*

The Sacrifice and the Substitute

From Genesis 15–22

One of God's best promises to Abram and his wife Sarai was to give them a giant family—as many children and grandchildren and great-grandchildren as there are stars in the sky! God was so committed to this promise that He changed Abram's name to Abraham, which means "father of many nations." And Sarai would now be Sarah, which means "princess." But there was a problem. Abraham and Sarah had no children, and they were old—I mean, *old* old.

God knew they were too old to have children, but He wanted everyone to know that this child was a miracle and a gift of His grace—something they didn't deserve and something that only the true God could do.

Sure enough, right on time, a son was born. They named him Isaac. Now, all of God's promises to Abraham could come true! *Maybe Isaac was the One.*

One day, when Isaac had grown up a lot, God spoke to Abraham again. *Abraham! Abraham! I want you to take your son,* God said, *your only son, the son you love, the one I promised you—and I want you to offer him to Me as a sacrifice.*

Could Abraham have misheard? Surely God wouldn't make him sacrifice his child—the one God had promised to give Abraham a giant family from. At that time, people sacrificed animals as a gift to God and a payment for their sins, but God would *never* ask them to sacrifice people.

Still, Abraham also knew what he heard. He knew God loved him, and he trusted God. So Abraham packed up his things and took the journey with Isaac to the mountain where he was to make the sacrifice. Abraham believed that, somehow, he would come back down from the mountain with Isaac because God doesn't take back His promises.

The two of them climbed and climbed until they reached the top. Abraham built an altar, put wood on it for a fire, bound his son, tied him to the altar, and just as he was ready to do the unspeakable . . . .

Stop! God spoke. *Do not lay a hand on your son! Now I know that you love Me and trust Me completely.* Abraham looked up, and he saw a ram. The ram was a substitute—it was supposed to trade places with Isaac.

Isaac wasn't sacrificed that day; instead, God gave a substitute. Abraham and Isaac's sin still needed to be paid for, just like it does for all of us. Like Adam and Eve, Noah, and Abraham, we don't trust God. And because of this, we deserve to be sent away from His presence and to pay the price for our sin—which is death.

But God doesn't take back His promises, and He doesn't give up on us because of our failures. He is determined to give us the unending life and unlimited love we were made for. For this to be possible, we need a substitute to pay for our sin.

There is One coming, God promised.
He's the One we're waiting for.

Song for family reflection:
"Rock of Ages"

Discuss these questions together

- *What does it teach you about God that He gave Abraham and Sarah a son, just like He promised?*
- *How was Abraham able to have faith that he would come back down the mountain with Isaac, even though he was told to sacrifice him?*
- *What do you think it means that we need a substitute? Who do you think can be your substitute?*

Playing Favorites

From Genesis 24–35

Isaac kept growing up, and God repeated to him the promise He had made to Isaac's father, Abraham: *I will bless you. I will be your God. You and your children and your children's children will be My people.*

Eventually, Isaac got married, and his wife Rebekah became pregnant with twin boys. In those days, it *really* mattered who was born first—even if it was just by two minutes! The firstborn son would be given the family blessing and more of the family's money. Isaac and Rebekah assumed that the oldest would also be given the blessing that God had given to Abraham and Isaac.

But God told Rebekah before she gave birth, *The older one will serve the younger*. God promised to do things differently than the way they were usually done. Being born first doesn't make you any better, and God said He was going to give the blessing to the younger one.

Now, I'm sure you've never fought with any of your brothers or sisters or with friends who are like your brothers and sisters, but these boys *were fighting from the moment they were born!* In fact, they were racing to see who could be born first! Though Esau was the firstborn, Jacob was holding onto his heel as tight as he could.

As these boys grew up, their parents started playing favorites (something parents should never do). Their dad loved Esau the most, and their mom loved Jacob the most. Esau was supposed to get the blessing—because he was the oldest and his dad's favorite. But Rebekah knew what God had told her. She also wanted *her* favorite child to get the blessing.

Just like Adam and Eve and Noah and everyone else, neither Jacob nor his mom Rebekah *really* trusted God. They thought God might take back His promise or take too long to keep it. So they came up with a sneaky plan to steal Esau's blessing.

Esau was a manly man, covered in hair. He was also a hunter who spent his days outside. Jacob preferred to stay inside with his mother. Jacob and Esau's dad Isaac was old, and he could barely see anything anymore. He was ready to give Esau his blessing, but Rebekah knew, because of his bad eyesight, Isaac could be tricked. So Rebekah said to Jacob, "Let's trick your father. Make him this meal he loves, put on some of Esau's clothes, and cover your arms and neck in goat hair—your father won't know the difference!"

The plan worked. Jacob and Rebekah tricked Isaac into blessing Jacob instead of Esau. After that, Esau hated Jacob so much that Jacob had to run away so Esau wouldn't kill him! Rebekah and Jacob's lying and cheating tore the family in two—and it tore Jacob's own heart in two as well.

But none of this had to happen. God had already promised Jacob the blessing. If Jacob had trusted God and waited on His timing, he would've been blessed without tearing his family apart. Jacob felt guilty and sad for the rest of his life. He spent his days doubting if God loved him and wanted to bless him and continuing to trick and lie and steal—and people did the same thing to him.

Jacob was not a good brother. He was a sneak and a cheat who stole his father's blessing from his brother. But there is One coming who is like a brother to all of God's children. He is a perfect brother—God's first-born Son. Instead of cheating and stealing God's blessing, He came to give us the blessing of unending life and unlimited love—even though it would cost Him *everything.*

There is One coming, God promised. He's the One we're waiting for.

Song for family reflection:

"He Will Hold Me Fast"

Discuss these questions together

- *Why did Jacob think he needed to steal the blessing? Do you ever doubt that God loves you and will bless you?*
- *What do you think it means for God to bless you?*
- *Who do you think is the older brother who came to give us unending life and unlimited love?*

Playing Favorites Again

From Genesis 37, 39–50

There was once a boy who was his dad's favorite—and *everyone* knew it.

You may be thinking, *Didn't we just learn that Esau was his dad's favorite?* That's right. This story starts with Esau's brother Jacob, who grew up knowing his brother was the favorite. Still, *Jacob played favorites with his kids too.* Jacob grew up and had lots of sons. In fact, he had twelve! And Joseph was his favorite.

To show his great love for Joseph, Jacob made him a beautiful coat that Joseph wore every day. You might even say he *flaunted* it or showed it off.

One day, Joseph's brothers had had enough. They were away from home working when Joseph came to them. When they saw him coming, they decided to get their revenge. They took off Joseph's fancy coat and sold him to slave traders. Then, they covered his coat in animal blood to make Jacob think his beloved son had died.

Joseph's situation only got worse. He was enslaved in the house of a rich Egyptian man, and then, he was unfairly sent to prison.

While in prison, God helped Joseph interpret dreams. If someone had a troubling dream, they would ask Joseph what it meant, and Joseph would tell them. One of the men Joseph interpreted a dream for was released from prison. He promised to put in a good word for Joseph with Pharaoh, the king of Egypt, so Joseph could get out of prison too. But the man forgot!

It might have seemed like that man wasn't the only one who had forgotten Joseph. Joseph probably thought God had forgotten him too. But one day, when Pharaoh had a bad dream, that man remembered Joseph. Pharoah sent for Joseph so he could tell him what the dream meant, and Joseph did! Pharaoh was so thrilled that he made Joseph his number-two man—like the vice president of Egypt (and Egypt was the most powerful country in the world). Would Joseph be the One?

While Joseph was the number-two man, a great famine came over the whole land—which meant there wasn't enough food for the people to eat. But the Egyptians had enough because God was with Joseph. One day, Jacob—Joseph's father—sent Joseph's brothers to Egypt to ask for food. Joseph immediately recognized them. "It's me," he said to them, "I'm your lost brother—the one you sold into slavery."

They were terrified. Can you imagine? What if you had done something so horrible, so awful, so terrible, *so* bad to your brother or sister, and then they became the second most powerful person in the world? But Joseph didn't want revenge. He protected them.

"What you did was evil," Joseph said, "but God meant it for good. He sent me here to Egypt so that when the famine came, you could come get enough food to survive." God sent Joseph there to make good on His promise to Abraham: unending life and unlimited love.

Joseph was not the One. In the end, he would die like everyone else. But one day, God would send another—a Son loved by His Father and rejected by His brothers. He wouldn't only be put in prison; He would die. But He wouldn't stay dead. Just as Joseph left the prison and was seated on a throne, the One we're waiting for would leave the prison of death and sit down on a throne as the King of everything.

There is One coming, God promised. He's the One we're waiting for.

Song for family reflection:

"O Love That Will Not Let Me Go"

Discuss these questions together

- *Why do you think Jacob grew up to make the same mistake his father made—the mistake that had been so hurtful to him?*
- *How would you have felt if you were Joseph, when things kept getting worse and worse?*
- *What does it tell you about God that, even though things looked so bad, His plan was still working and His promise was still true?*

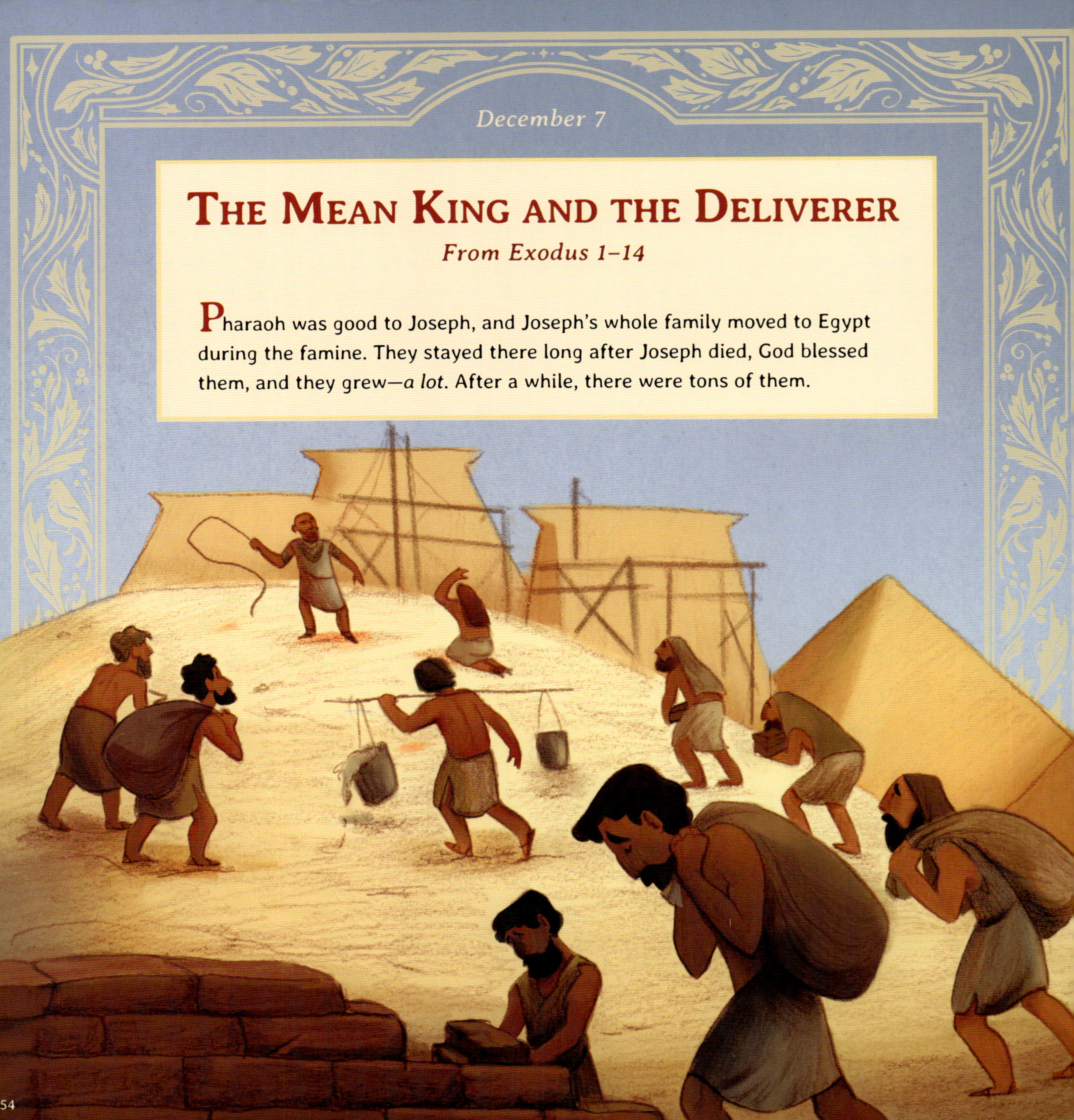

December 7

The Mean King and the Deliverer

From Exodus 1–14

Pharaoh was good to Joseph, and Joseph's whole family moved to Egypt during the famine. They stayed there long after Joseph died, God blessed them, and they grew—*a lot*. After a while, there were tons of them.

But there was a new Pharaoh in town. He didn't know Joseph, and he did not like Joseph's people. He was afraid of them. So what did Pharaoh do? He made them slaves and made their lives *miserable*. They had to work all day in the hot, hot Egyptian sun. And if they did anything wrong? Well, they'd have to work even harder!

The people felt like God had completely left them and forgotten all His promises—the promises of unending life and unlimited love. But God hadn't forgotten. They cried out to God, and He heard His people.

God raised up a man named Moses, and He told Moses to go to Pharaoh. *Give him this message for me*, God said. *Let my people go.* Moses did what God said (after a little arguing), but Pharaoh refused. He didn't know God. He certainly didn't trust God. He only trusted in himself.

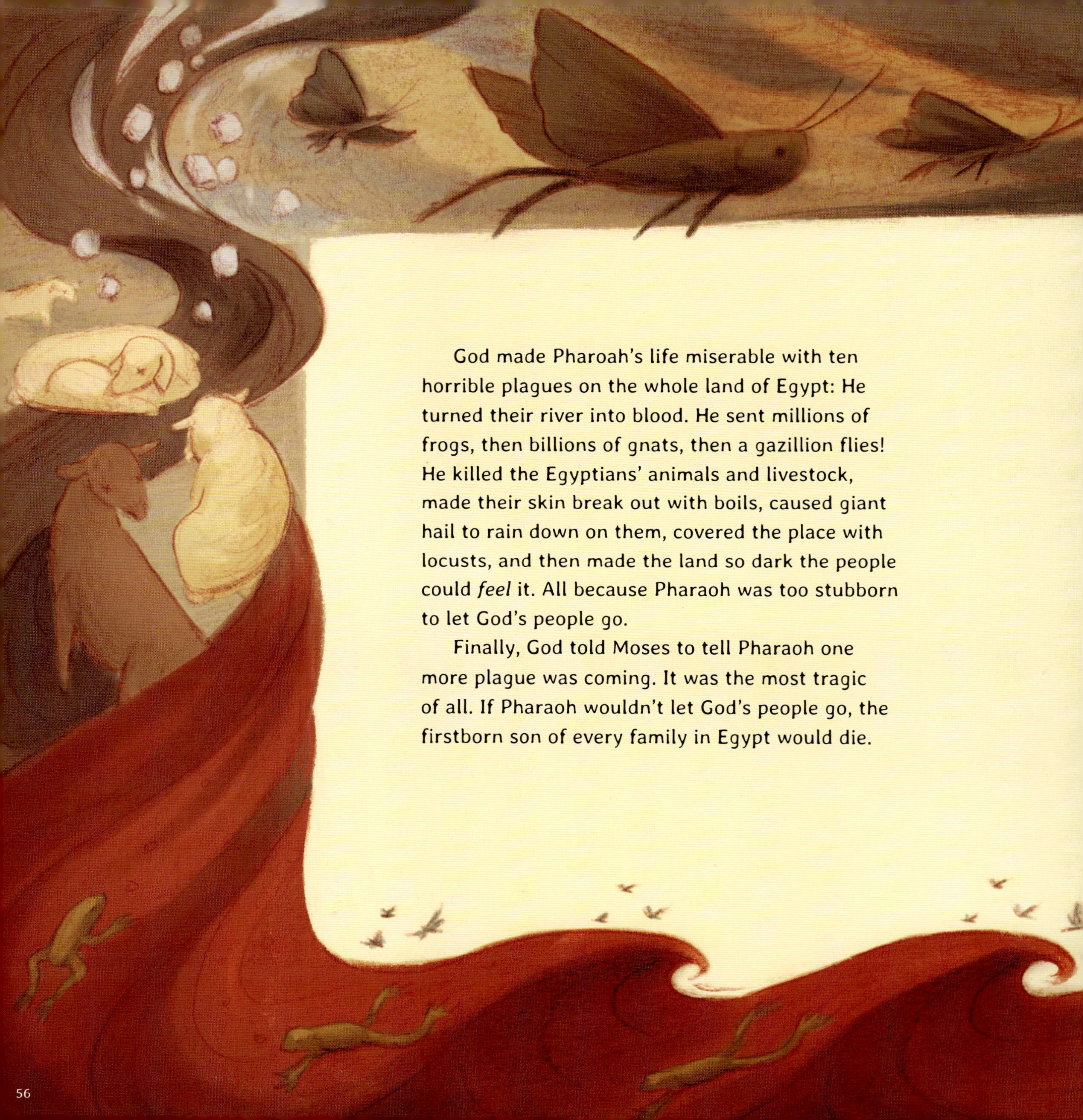

God made Pharoah's life miserable with ten horrible plagues on the whole land of Egypt: He turned their river into blood. He sent millions of frogs, then billions of gnats, then a gazillion flies! He killed the Egyptians' animals and livestock, made their skin break out with boils, caused giant hail to rain down on them, covered the place with locusts, and then made the land so dark the people could *feel* it. All because Pharaoh was too stubborn to let God's people go.

Finally, God told Moses to tell Pharaoh one more plague was coming. It was the most tragic of all. If Pharaoh wouldn't let God's people go, the firstborn son of every family in Egypt would die.

But the sons of the Israelites (that's a long word for Abraham's family) would be spared, if they sacrificed a lamb and painted their doorposts with its blood.

Pharaoh still refused. The moment came. The firstborn sons of the Egyptians died. But God passed over the Israelites. Their sons lived.

Pharaoh and the Egyptians were devastated. "Get out of here! We don't ever want to see you again," they shouted. But Pharaoh was still so hard-hearted that he changed his mind.

"Wait," he said to his army. "Go after them!"

The Egyptian army chased God's people, but Moses led the people, and God saved them. He parted the waters of a giant sea so the Israelites could walk across it on dry land. The moment the Egyptians arrived, God made the water come crashing down and swallow up their horses and their chariots.

God used Moses to save—or deliver—His people from slavery. But there was (and still is) a much stronger kind of slavery—the slavery to sin. God's people needed someone to free them from sin so they could trust Him. There's only One who can—the One God's people were waiting for. He would one day come, and the land would be so dark that people could feel it. Then, He—like the firstborn sons of Egypt—would die. But His death would be like the death of the sacrificial lamb, and all whose lives are covered by Him will be free—free from sin and free to enter unending life and unlimited love.

There is One coming, God promised. He's the One we're waiting for.

Song for family reflection:
"How Deep the Father's Love"

Discuss these questions together

- *How do you think you would've felt if you were an Israelite in slavery? How would you have felt when you were freed?*
- *What do you think it means that we are "in slavery to sin"?*
- *Why does there have to be a substitute and a sacrifice for us to be freed from slavery to sin?*

December 8

Rules, Rules, Rules

From Exodus 19–40, Leviticus, Deuteronomy

After God rescued His people from slavery in Egypt, He wanted to give them a new way to live as free people—His people. He wanted them to have a way to really experience the unending life and unlimited love He created them for.

How would God do this? By giving them a law.

Do you know what a "law" is? A law is a rule or a set of rules someone gives you to obey. You might say that your parents have a "law" for your home: clean up your toys after playing; share well with your brothers and sisters; be respectful to grown-ups; obey your mom and dad. You may sometimes think these rules are too much or aren't fair, but if everyone in the house followed the rules, everyone's life would be better! The same was true of God's rules. Just like He gave Adam and Eve rules, He would give His people rules, and as they followed them, their lives would be good.

One day, while the people were wandering through the desert between Egypt and the Promised Land, God called Moses up on a mountain, and He wrote down the laws for Moses to bring back to the people. Laws like this: don't give your heart to any other god; be respectful to your parents; don't take what doesn't belong to you; always tell the truth.

God gave them laws about how to worship Him (like “a priest will make sacrifices for your forgiveness”), laws about how to treat others (like “love your neighbor as yourself” and “care for the poor among you”), and laws about all kinds of other things like what to eat, how to dress, and what to do if you’re sick.

God's law was very good, and if the people would obey it, God said things would go very well for them.

Only, they didn't obey it. They didn't obey it *at all*.

Just like Adam and Eve, they trusted themselves instead of trusting God.

And you know what happens when you don't obey the law, right? Of course, you do. There are consequences.

When Adam and Eve sinned by trusting themselves more than God and breaking His rules, they had to leave the garden, and they lost the unending life and unlimited love they were made for. Sadly, God's people—the very people He had so amazingly rescued from Egypt—acted just like Adam and Eve. They broke God's law and missed out on the life and love God wanted for them.

God still has a law, and just like His people in this story, all people fail to obey it. We deserve consequences for our disobedience and sin. But there is one Person—and only one—who obeyed God's law perfectly. He would come into the world and obey every single one of God's laws. But then He would receive the punishment and consequence that other people deserved for breaking the law! Why? So that they could have the unending life and unlimited love He deserved.

There is One coming, God promised. He's the One we're waiting for.

Song for family reflection:

"Holy, Holy, Holy"

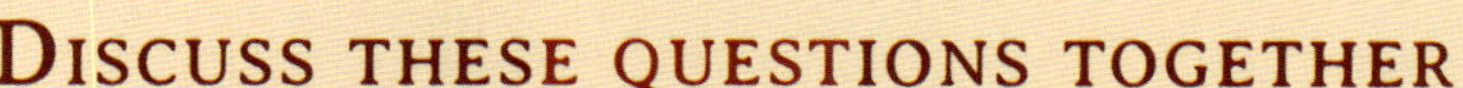

Discuss these questions together

- *Why do you think God gave His people a law? Was it to make their lives better or worse?*
- *Why do you think the people didn't obey God's law?*
- *Do you obey God's law?*

God's Griping, Grumbling People

From Exodus 16–17, Numbers 21

The Israelites—Abraham's family—were finally getting ready to go back to the special land God had promised their great-great-great-great-grandfather Abraham long ago.

Do you remember Abraham, whose name used to be Abram? Remember how God came to him one day out of nowhere and started making promises left and right? *I'm going to give you a son! I'm going to give you as many grandkids as there are stars! I'm going to be your God, and your kids and their kids and their kids will all be My people!*

One of the promises God made was that He would give Abraham and his family a home—a special land. There, they would live, and God would live with them. It would be almost like a brand-new garden of Eden.

Abraham's family traveled to this land, but when famine came, they had to go to Egypt, and well, you remember how that turned out. They ended up in slavery for hundreds of years! But now that God had freed them, He promised, *I'm taking you back to the Promised Land.*

But it was taking a while.

The Israelites probably felt like you might feel during a very, very long car ride to a family vacation. They were excited to get there but ready to get the traveling part over with. And so, they started complaining.

God still loved them. He was kind to them. He provided everything they needed. But they kept complaining still.

They complained, “We’re hungry!” God responded by making manna—a kind of magical heavenly bread—fall from the sky onto the land. They had so much they couldn’t eat it all!

They griped, “We’re thirsty!” God told Moses to hit a rock with his staff. When Moses did, water gushed out of the rock—enough for all the Israelites to drink!

They grumbled, “We’re miserable! God should have just left us in Egypt.” This is when God decided it was time to punish the Israelites for their complaining. He had been patient, but it was time for a consequence. God sent poisonous snakes into their camp! Many people got sick and even died when the snakes bit them.

The people realized how sinful they had been by not trusting God and complaining even though God had provided for them. They went to Moses and said they were sorry. "Pray for us," they pleaded, "and ask God to make the snakes go away." God heard His people and told Moses to make a metal snake and put it on a tall pole. Anyone who looked up at the snake would be healed.

Just like God provided water from the rock and manna from heaven, and just as God kept all the promises He'd made to Abram all those years before, God brought healing into the Israelites' camp through the snake on a pole. But the snake, water, and manna couldn't provide unending life or unlimited love.

They were pointing forward to something—Someone—else. This Someone would give people water for their souls, be the Bread of Life, and be raised up, not on metal, but on wood. Anyone who looked at Him would be healed not just from their sick bodies, but from their sick and sinful hearts.

There is One coming, God promised.
He's the One we're waiting for.

Song for family reflection:

"My Hope Is Built on Nothing Less"

Discuss these questions together

- *What's something you sometimes complain about? Why do you think people complain about things?*
- *If we completely trusted God, would we still complain? Why or why not?*
- *What do you think it means that God promised to send Someone to be "raised up" and give people unending life and unlimited love?*

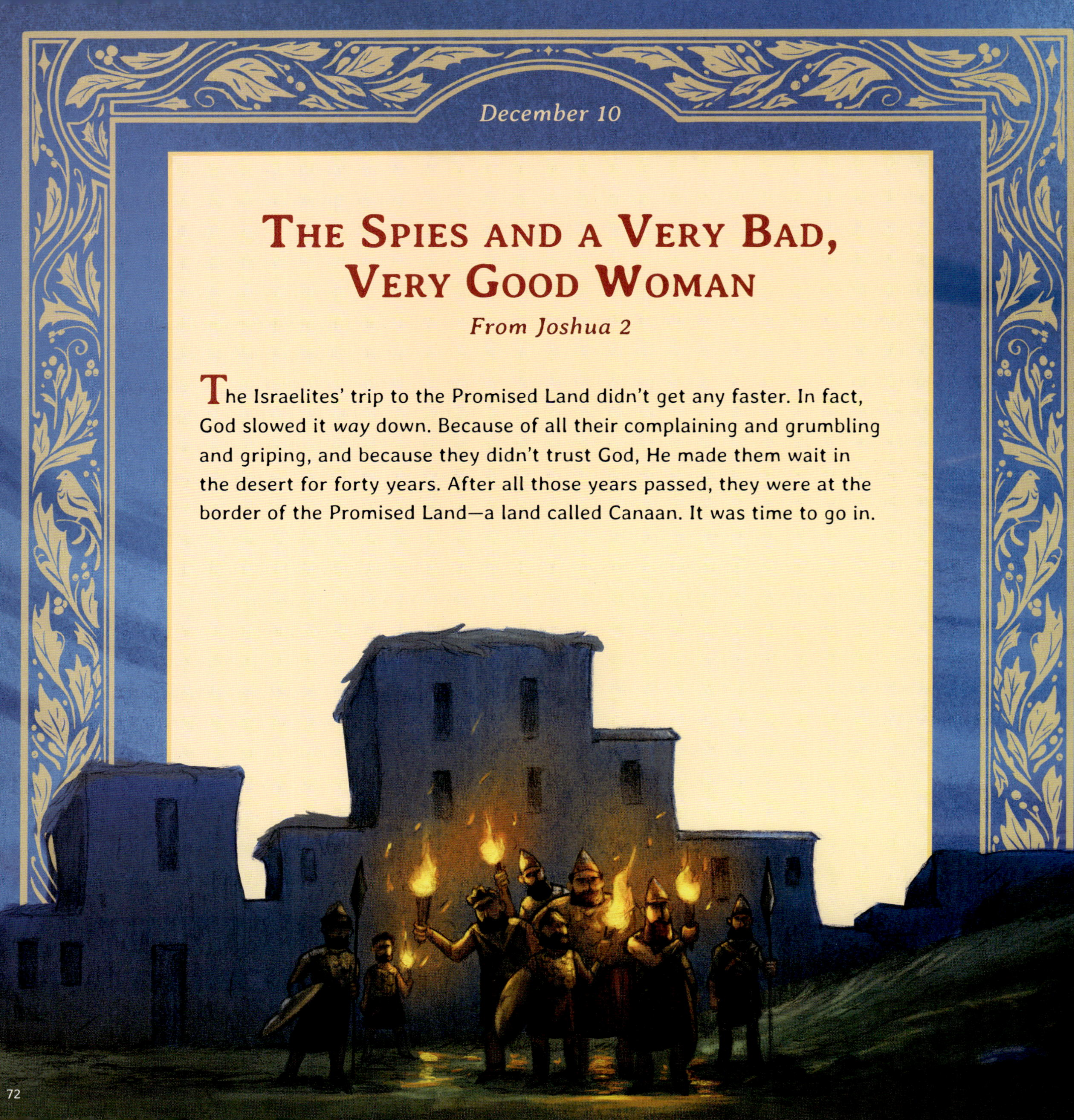

December 10

The Spies and a Very Bad, Very Good Woman

From Joshua 2

The Israelites' trip to the Promised Land didn't get any faster. In fact, God slowed it *way* down. Because of all their complaining and grumbling and griping, and because they didn't trust God, He made them wait in the desert for forty years. After all those years passed, they were at the border of the Promised Land—a land called Canaan. It was time to go in.

The Israelites had a new leader, Joshua, who replaced Moses. Joshua chose two men to sneak into the land as spies. They needed to see what the place was like and what the people were like who were already there. It was not good news. The people were very bad—so bad that if they had even learned the two spies were there, they would have killed them!

The two spies needed protection —somewhere to hide. And they found it in an unlikely place: the home of who they thought of as a VERY BAD woman.

This woman's name was Rahab, and she had a bad reputation. (*Reputation* is a big word that means "what other people think about you.") Everyone knew she was trouble.

But Rahab had heard about God. She'd learned about His great power, how He had freed His people from Egypt, and how He had defeated many other armies in the dessert. She knew about His unending love and how He had chosen Abraham's family to be His people and would do anything for them. And even though she had done many VERY BAD things, she thought in her heart, *I want to be on God's side*. So she offered to protect the spies by giving them a hiding place.

"Stay in here," she told them. "I'll tell my people that you left a long time ago."

When the coast was clear, the two spies left with a promise to reward her. "When we come in and take the Promised Land," they said, "you and anyone else in your house will be safe, and you can become a part of God's chosen people. Put a scarlet rope in your window so we know that it's you."

Sure enough, God's people came to the land, and God gave it to them. Rahab put the rope in the window, she and her family were safe, and they joined God's people. God loves people who have done VERY BAD things and have a VERY BAD reputation. He wants to use people like that to give His people the unending life and unlimited love they were made for!

Many years later, Rahab would be the great-grandmother of royalty. And many, many, many years later, her great-great-great-great-grandson would remind God's people of Rahab. But He would be even better. While Rahab protected the spies from her people, He would protect us from the punishment we deserve for our sin. While she helped God's people get into God's Promised Land, He would make a way for God's people to get into a place that will be better than Canaan and even better than Eden. While God's people knew Rahab by her scarlet rope, this One would be known by the scarlet blood He'd spill for our sins.

There is One coming, God promised. He's the One we're waiting for.

Song for family reflection:

"Nothing but the Blood of Jesus"

Discuss these questions together

- *Does it surprise you that God loves VERY BAD people?*
- *Do you think some people are better than others, or are we all VERY BAD people in need of God's love and grace?*
- *What do you think is the "better place" that the One we're waiting for will take us to?*

Follow the Leader

From Joshua 6

When Moses died, God called Joshua to Himself and said, *It's time for you to lead the people into the Promised Land.*

But of course, it wouldn't be easy. In fact, there were two big barriers in the way: a rushing river and a powerful city surrounded by giant walls.

The rushing river was the River Jordan, and it stood directly between the people and the Promised Land. *How will we cross?* the people wondered.

They had way too many people, too many animals, and too many possessions to swim through it, and going around it would take forever. But the God who told them to cross was the same God who spoke the world into creation, the same God who gave a miraculous child to childless Sarah, and the same God who parted the Red Sea so the Israelites could flee from Egypt. What was a rushing river to Him?

One morning, God told Joshua to command the priests carrying the ark of the covenant (a beautifully decorated box where God's presence stayed with the people) to go and stand in the Jordan. Joshua obeyed, and as soon as the ark got to the water, the rushing river stopped. The water piled up on one side of the people, and dry land appeared—just as it had on the way out of Egypt! Through water, the people were freed from slavery; through water, they came into the Promised Land.

After this, there was one more big problem: a powerful city called Jericho, full of strong, mean, nasty warriors, and a big, tall wall blocking the Israelites from getting into the city. The people were terrified. How would they ever defeat such a strong army—especially with such a big barrier in their way?

But God was still with them, and He promised to deliver them. Again, He gave Joshua instructions: *First, go up to Jericho and march around the city six days in a row. On the seventh day, take seven horns, carry the ark, and walk around the city seven times. After the seventh time, blow the horns, and yell really loud.*

Wait, what? The people must have been confused. *That* was the plan? Walk around the city and make a bunch of noise? Surely the warriors inside the city walls would laugh at the Israelites. They wouldn't be intimidated by something that looked and sounded so silly.

Sometimes, God uses plans that seem ridiculous to us, but they work just to show us that He is the One who saves. We cannot save ourselves. The people obeyed this seemingly ridiculous plan, and sure enough, the walls came tumbling down.

God raised up this man Joshua, just like He had raised up Moses to lead His people into the Promised Land. Finally, the people were where they were supposed to be! They had seen God fulfill His promises, split waters in two, and take down monstrous walls with the sound of trumpets. Surely, they would follow God's law and all would be good again, right?

But Joshua wasn't the One. Eventually, the people stopped listening to him, and they stopped obeying God's law—bringing about disastrous consequences. Joshua points us to another leader. In fact, Joshua's name in his language, *Yeshua*, means "rescuer" or "deliverer." He points us to the great Rescuer and Deliver who would rescue us from our sins and bring us into the true Promised Land—the land of unending life and unlimited love.

There is One coming, God promised. He's the One we're waiting for.

Song for family reflection:

"On Jordan's Stormy Banks I Stand"

Discuss these questions together

- *Who are some leaders in your life—people you follow and obey?*
- *What do you think made Joshua such a great leader?*
- *What kind of leader or deliverer would it take to save us from our sin? Do you think any leader could be strong enough to do that?*

The Strong Man Who Gave Away His Strength

From Judges 13–16

After God gave Abraham's family the Promised Land, their leader Joshua grew old and died. But instead of remembering all the amazing things God had done for them, the people turned their hearts away from God. They trusted in themselves instead of God, and bad things happened to them—just as God said. Their enemies attacked the land from every side.

It happened over and over again: The people would forget about God and trust their own hearts; they would be attacked and overtaken by their enemies; and then they would remember God and cry out for help. Each time, God raised up a deliverer called a "judge" to save them. Then, they would turn their hearts away from Him all over again!

One of the judges God raised to save His people was a man named Samson. Samson was the strongest man around. So strong that one time, he fought a lion with his bare hands . . . and won!

But Samson wasn't a bodybuilder or an Olympic weight lifter. His strength was a gift straight from God. God wanted Samson to keep his faith in God and not in his strong arms, so God told Samson that if he ever cut his hair, his strength would be lost.

Well, Samson thought quite a lot of himself, and over time, he became foolish and prideful. (*Pride* is a short but important word that means thinking you are the best and can fix your problems on your own without help). Samson told a beautiful woman the secret of his hair. That woman went and told the enemies of God's people. And they sent her back to make sure his hair was cut off.

The moment Samson's hair was chopped, his strength was gone, just as God said. He was arrested by God's enemies, tied up, mocked, spit on, and made fun of. The people of God had lost their rescuer—now what would happen to them? God's enemies celebrated and praised their own not-real god for giving Samson over to them.

Even though God's people were wicked, and Samson was full of pride, God did not leave them. One day, while in the custody of the evil enemies, Samson cried out to God and received his strength back. He stood in the middle of the enemies' temple, stretched his arms out, and pushed down the pillars that supported the building. The ceiling came crashing down on all of them—Samson included. In one last moment of strength, Samson delivered Israel—even though it cost him his life.

Samson was foolish, prideful, and not the One. But God would soon send Someone else stronger than a bodybuilder, Olympic weight lifter, and even stronger than Samson. He would be more powerful than we can imagine. Yet He, too, would lose His strength—not because it was taken from Him, but because He gave it up willingly. And in one last moment of might, He would stretch his arms out and give up His life to save God's people from the greatest enemy of all.

There is One coming, God promised. He's the One we're waiting for.

Song for family reflection:

"Lord, I Need You"

Discuss these questions together

- *Where did Samson's strength really come from? From himself? From his hair? Or from something or Someone else?*
- *What does "pride" mean? Why do you think Samson acted so pridefully? Do you ever act pridefully?*
- *What kind of person would willingly give up their strength to save other people?*

A Ray of Hope

From Ruth

The time when Samson lived—the time of the judges—was bad. I mean, *really* bad. God created His people for unending life and unlimited love, but what they were experiencing was more like unending death and unlimited darkness.

That's what happens when we trust our own hearts more than we trust God. We begin to think we know best about what kind of people we should be, how we should live, the things we should love, and the way we should treat others. The Israelites thought they knew best, and things got worse and worse and worse.

It was almost completely hopeless, almost completely dark.

Almost.

But there is one story that shines like a bright ray of hope.

There was a woman named Ruth who was not from Abraham's family, but her husband was. When Ruth's husband died, his mother decided to go back to the Promised Land and live among God's people. Even though Ruth was not an Israelite, she courageously left everything she knew and went with her mother-in-law, Naomi, to follow the one true God.

Since both Ruth and Naomi's husbands had died, they were widows. In those days, being a widow meant you probably didn't have much money, and you might be in danger of bad men. Because of this, Ruth had to go find her own food in the fields. One day, she just so happened to wander into a field owned by a man named Boaz.

When Boaz learned that Ruth was a widow, he made sure that all the men in his field protected Ruth, and that no one said or did anything mean to her. Then, he went to find out who she was. Turns out, Boaz was a relative of Ruth's husband, who had died. And the laws at the time said that he could be her "Kinsman-Redeemer," or someone who could marry a widow and make sure she would no longer be poor or in danger. That's exactly what Boaz did.

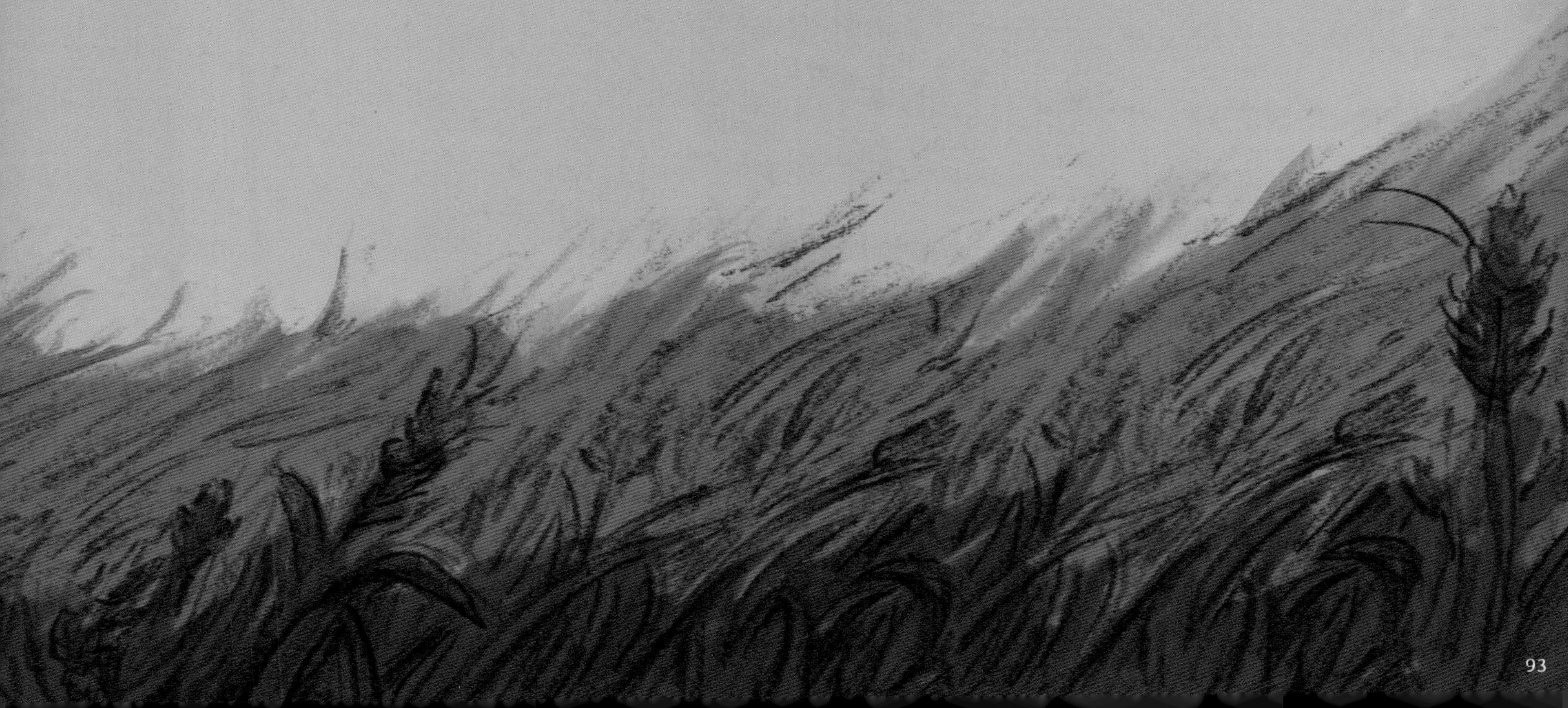

We all need a Kinsman-Redeemer: someone who is noble, does the right thing, and is willing to sacrifice so our hearts are no longer in danger. Boaz redeemed his wife, Ruth, who was from a different nation outside of God's people. But soon, Someone else would come to redeem people from every tribe, tongue, and nation.

Boaz and Ruth would have a baby, who would grow up and have a baby, who would have another baby, and that baby would become king over all of Israel. And that king would have children and grandchildren, and one of his great-great-great-great-grandchildren would be the great Kinsman-Redeemer God promised way back in the beginning.

There is One coming, God promised. He's the One we're waiting for.

Song for family reflection:

"Anchor of Hope"

Discuss these questions together

- *How would you describe Ruth? What about Boaz? How did God use them in His story?*
- *God was still working even in the darkest and hardest of times. What does this tell you about God?*
- *What kind of redeemer do we really need? What do we need to be redeemed from?*

The Woman Who Prayed for a Son

From 1 Samuel 1

A couple hundred years after Ruth lived, another important woman came along. Her name was Hannah.

Hannah was very sad. There was something she wanted more than anything else, and she didn't have it. Hannah wanted a baby. And even though it seemed like everyone around her had lots of babies, she hadn't become pregnant.

In Hannah's day, people believed that if a woman didn't have children, God must not love her or care about her! (Of course, this wasn't true, but Hannah didn't know.) Hannah thought this about herself—that the reason she couldn't have a baby was because God must have forgotten all about her.

But even though she was sad, Hannah prayed. Then she prayed some more. And then she kept praying and didn't stop.

One day, Hannah was crying and pouring out her heart to God. “Remember me, and do not forget me,” she begged God. Of course, God had never forgotten her. He always remembered her, and He had always loved her.

What Hannah didn't know is that just because other people don't love you or think you are special doesn't mean that God doesn't love you and care for you.

To show Hannah that He loved her and heard her prayer, God told a priest—an important spiritual leader—to speak to Hannah and tell her that God would answer her prayer. Like Abraham and Sarah, who wanted children but didn't have any because they were too old, Hannah would miraculously have a son, and he would be special, set apart from others.

Sure enough, just like with Abraham and Sarah, Hannah had a son. She named him Samuel, which means something like, "I asked the Lord for you."

Samuel was set apart. He grew up to be one of the most important Israelites ever. He loved God, and God spoke with him. God made him a leader of the people, a prophet who spoke God's Word, a priest who led the people in their worship of God, and even the one who appointed the first kings of Israel!

Samuel was set apart to help point people to God. He, like Isaac, was born because of a miracle done by God for a woman who could not have children. But there was another miraculous birth coming. Another woman who could not have children would also have a son.

He would be the greatest, most important leader among God's people. He would speak God's Word and lead people to worship God. He wouldn't just appoint kings; He would be *the* King! *The One*! And He would bring unending life and unlimited love to God's people.

There is One coming, God promised.
He's the One we're waiting for.

Song for family reflection:
"Before the Throne of God Above"

Discuss these questions together

- *Did God love Hannah even when she thought He didn't? What does this tell you about God's love for you?*
- *Does God always answer our prayers? Why or why not? How can we trust God's plans even when it feels like He doesn't answer our prayers?*
- *Why do you think God keeps writing stories about miraculous births? Why do His stories point to one another?*

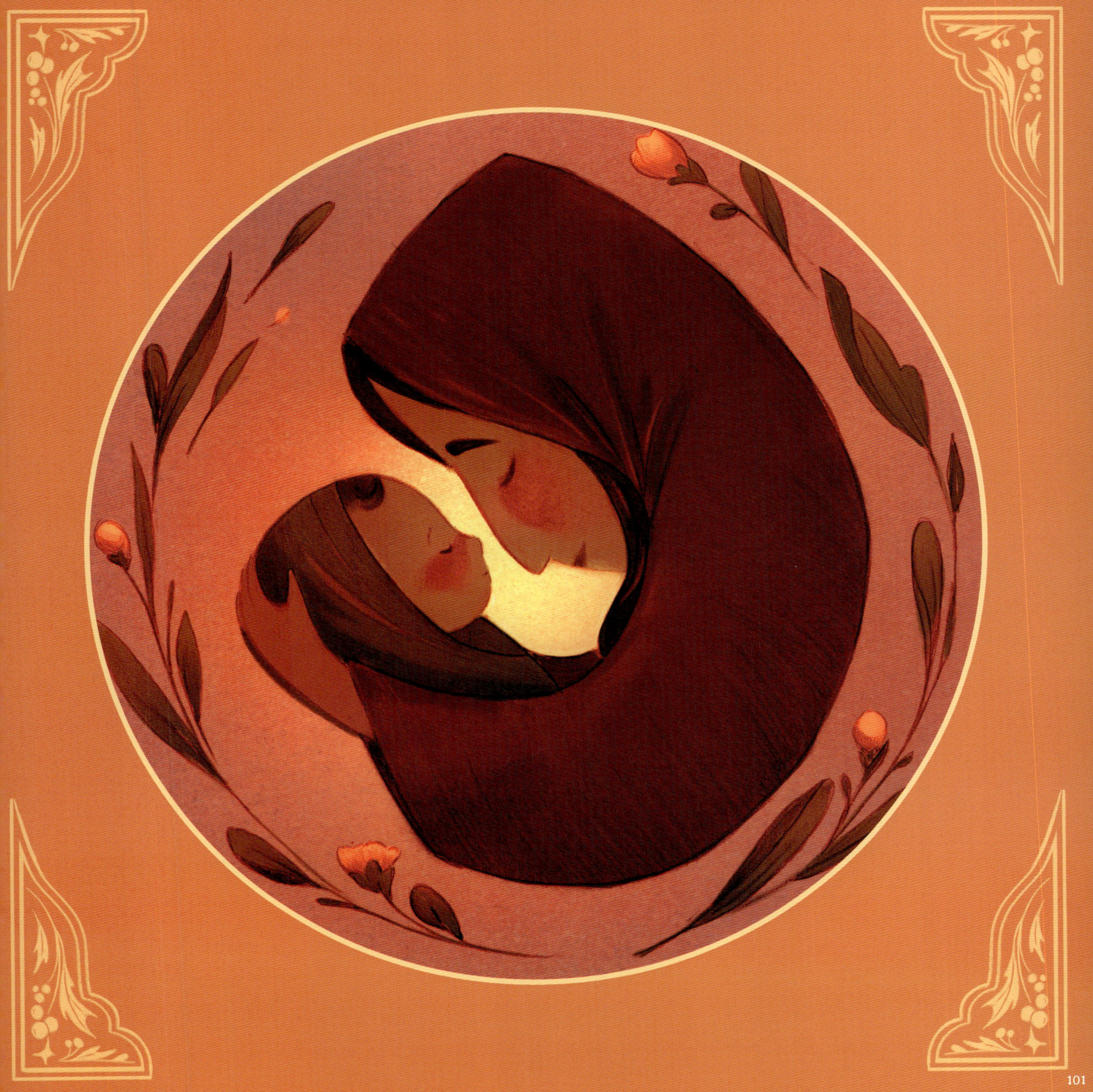

God Picks an Unimpressive King

From 1 Samuel 16:1–13

Imagine that one day, a mysterious messenger knocks on your door and asks for you.

"I'm coming with an important order from the high courts of great power," says the messenger. "You—*yes, you*—are being given the most important job imaginable. *You* are to choose the next king of your country." You would be shocked! Amazed! Flabbergasted! (Which is a word that means the same thing as "shocked" and "amazed" but is longer and funnier.)

After you settled down, you'd get to work. What would you do first? Perhaps you would make a list of everything you would look for in your king. What would be on your list? Do you want him to be wise? Kind? Generous? Should he be tall, strong, and powerful? Should he be the richest person in the land?

When Samuel—Hannah's son—grew up, he was God's messenger, called a prophet. He told the people what God wanted them to know. The people told Samuel to tell God they wanted a king. They were no longer happy with just having God as their king—they wanted a king they could see, just like all the other nations.

So God gave them the kind of king they wanted.

Israel's first king was a man named Saul—the kind of man the Israelites thought would be a great king. He was tall, strong, and powerful—impressive in every way! He was also selfish and cared more about himself than about the people he ruled. He didn't love or listen to God, and he certainly couldn't bring the people into the unending life and unlimited love they were made for. Saul's reign was an absolute disaster.

Saul was so prideful that God planned to take the kingdom away from him. God told Samuel, *I want you to go and find the next king for My people. This king will be the kind of king that I want—a man after My own heart.*

God led Samuel to the home of a man named Jesse. Jesse had eight sons. With each one Samuel saw, he thought, *This must be the king!* The first one passed by—strong and tall and handsome. But God said, *This isn't the one.* The second passed by. The third. The fourth. All of them had the kind of qualities you would put on your list! But every time, God said, *This isn't the one.*

God taught Samuel a very important lesson that day. *People do not see what I see,* God told him. *People look at outward appearances, but I look at the heart.*

Finally, after Samuel had seen seven sons, he asked Jesse, "Do you have any more?"

"Well," said Jesse, "there's one more—but it can't be him. He's the youngest, smallest, and most unimpressive in every way. He's just a little shepherd boy and musician!" But as soon as Samuel laid eyes on him—David was his name—God said, *This is the one.*

David was indeed a king after God's own heart. Though he made mistakes and had failures along the way, he was the greatest king in the history of God's people. But he wasn't *the* King—he wasn't *the* One.

Just like David, this One would be small and unimpressive to people's eyes. Nothing about Him would make us think that He could bring us unlimited love and unending life. In fact, no one would think He could be the King who would save God's people! No one, that is, except God.

There is One coming, God promised. He's the One we're waiting for.

Song for family reflection:

"Once in Royal David's City"

Discuss these questions together

- *Why do you think the qualities we would look for in a king or leader are so different from what God looks for?*
- *What does it mean that people look at outward appearances but God looks at the heart?*
- *Why do you think God would choose a leader for His people who was so unimpressive to everyone else?*

David and the Nasty Giant

From 1 Samuel 17

I want you to try something with me. Now, it might not be very pleasant, but let's go for it anyway. Can you name some things that scare you?

Loud thunderstorms?

The dark?

New people?

Big, barking dogs?

Eating your vegetables?

We're all afraid of something—even the biggest, strongest, bravest people get scared! But there was once a man so big, so strong, so mean, so ugly, so loud, and so—well, so *scary*—that everyone who saw him was terrified of him. That man's name was *Goliath*.

Goliath was an enemy of God's people. But not just any ordinary enemy. Goliath was a *giant*. (Literally. He was three feet taller than the next tallest guy!) And this big, strong, mean, ugly, loud, scary, giant enemy of God's people would walk out every day and make fun of God's people.

"You're all a bunch of scaredy-cats! Send out your strongest man—he's no match for me! Your whole army can't triumph over me. Your strongest warrior can't beat me! Even your God can't defeat me."

His taunting worked. All of God's people were terrified.

All of them, that is, except one.

Do you remember David, the little boy that God said would be king? Well, not long after Samuel told him he would be king (but before he actually was king), David was home tending his sheep. Three of his brothers—who were bigger and stronger than David—were out fighting against the Philistines, the enemies of God's people, and the army of Goliath. David's dad told him to take some supplies to his brothers on the battlefield, so he loaded up his things and went. But when he got there, he was shocked at what he found.

Everyone was shaking in their boots, too afraid to fight! Goliath was mocking the people, taunting and yelling at them, and they were all huddled up like babies in the corner!

But David was not afraid. "What's wrong with you all?" he asked. "Sure, Goliath may be bigger and stronger than us, but we have the living God on our side. No one can defeat Him!"

David knew that with God on his side, Goliath was no match. So he took his trusty slingshot, loaded up a few stones, and walked out to meet Goliath.

What must have gone through Goliath's head when this little kid came out to meet him? *A child!? This is going to be too easy!* But all it took was one stone in David's sling. One shot. David picked up his stone, put it in his slingshot, and slung it—*whoosh!*—at the giant. It landed—*thwack!*—right on the giant's forehead.

A confused look came over Goliath's face. He began to lose his footing. The world around him spun and spun until finally, he tumbled down to the ground with a great *crash!* Goliath was dead. The big, strong, mean, ugly, loud, scary, giant, unbeatable enemy was beaten.

David knew God could defeat even the strongest, scariest enemies. But you and I need to be saved from an enemy much stronger than a giant. We need to be saved from our sin. Saved from the devil. Saved from death itself! The good news? Someone was coming who would save us from even these great enemies. He wouldn't need a giant on His side; He wouldn't need a huge army; He wouldn't even need a slingshot and stone. He'd just need Himself.

There is One coming, God promised. He's the One we're waiting for.

Song for family reflection:

"Hail to the Lord's Anointed"

Discuss these questions together

- *What are some of the things you said you were scared of? Do you think God is stronger than those scary things?*
- *How did David defeat Goliath?*
- *What do you think it means that our greatest enemies are sin, the devil, and death? How can these enemies be defeated?*

The Wisest Man Who Ever Lived

From 1 Kings 1–11

King David was a king after God's own heart. But like every other leader before him, his time came to an end. After him, his son Solomon became king.

One day, God asked Solomon a question that every person would like to be asked: *What do you want?* God promised to give Solomon whatever he asked for.

What would you say if God asked you that question? What would you like more than anything in the world? Money? Fame? Donuts for breakfast and chocolate cake for dessert every day for the rest of your life?

Solomon's answer might surprise you. "I would like wisdom," he told God. Which was a very *wise* answer. God kept His promise—as He always does—and made Solomon the wisest man in the world (*and* the richest).

Under King Solomon the Wise, the kingdom of Israel grew to new heights. Other nations all around saw how God was blessing Israel! King Solomon's leadership made them healthy, wealthy, and famous. Not only did Solomon rule and reign over his kingdom with wisdom, he also taught his people how to be wise. He wrote many great wisdom sayings—some of which are in the Bible! It seemed like the people were getting a taste of the unending life and unlimited love God promised them.

But Solomon didn't keep using God's wisdom. Even though God gave Solomon wisdom, Solomon turned away from it. Worse, he turned away from God. Solomon found out that all the wisdom in the world isn't worth much if you don't use it. He listened to his heart rather than God's Word.

Like Adam and Eve and so many people before him, Solomon began to act like he knew more than God—which is what he used to call foolishness, the opposite of true wisdom! He married lots of women who worshiped other gods, started worshiping those gods himself, and loved money more than God or other people. The wisest man who ever lived became a fool, and his great kingdom came tumbling down.

Solomon's turn from God's wisdom didn't have consequences just for him, but for the whole kingdom he ruled. His foolishness caused the kingdom to fall apart, and at the end of his reign, Israel was torn in two. A civil war broke out, as brothers fought against brothers, family against family, neighbor against neighbor, and friend against friend.

It is a tragic thing when leaders turn away from God's wisdom and a wonderful thing when kings and rulers and leaders listen to God's wisdom. But even the wisest leaders make terrible mistakes. What we need is not just a leader who knows all the right things to do; what we need is a leader who will do them, all the time, without fail! A leader who has the wisdom to know what is right and the courage to do it! A leader who knows that God knows best and does everything God says. A leader who doesn't only write down God's wisdom but *is* God's wisdom—because He is God. Thankfully, that's exactly the kind of leader God promised to send.

There is One coming, God promised. He's the One we're waiting for.

Song for family reflection:
"Come Behold the Wondrous Mystery"

Discuss these questions together

- *Why do you think Solomon asked for wisdom instead of money, power, fame, or something else (like chocolate cake)?*
- *Why do you think even people who* know *the wise thing to do often don't do it? Do you ever choose to do the wrong thing even though you know what the right thing is?*
- *Who do you think is the leader who will be perfectly wise and lead God's people into unending life and unlimited love?*

A Good Man Who Lost Everything

From Job

A long time ago, there lived a man who had *everything.*

This man did not belong to the family of Abraham, but he did know and love God, and God knew and loved him. He worshiped God, obeyed God, and lived—the best he could—the way God wanted him to live. Was *he* the One?

It just so happened that he was also successful, rich, and happy. He had a beautiful family, many businesses, a large house, and tons of people working for him.

That is, until he didn't.

The man's name was Job. And one day, when he was just minding his business, several of his workers, one after the other, rushed to him with tragic news. The first said, "All of your oxen and donkeys were stolen by criminals, and they killed your servants! I'm the only one who escaped to tell you!"

Job had barely caught his breath when another messenger came rushing to him. "Fire fell from heaven and burned up all your sheep and the shepherds watching them! I'm the only one who escaped to tell you!"

He was still speaking when a third messenger rushed to Job. "Another group of criminals came and stole all your camels and killed more servants! I'm the only one who escaped to tell you!"

Imagine how Job must have felt. Staggering. Out of breath. All of his success, his wealth, and his livelihood was lost. Perhaps the thought entered his mind, *At least I still have my family*. But before he could say the words, a fourth messenger came: "Your sons and daughters were all together eating and drinking, and a strong wind blew into their house. I'm the only one who survived to tell you."

Still, that wasn't all. Job's body became covered with horrible sores, and he got very sick.

How would you have responded if you were Job? Would you be angry? Heartbroken? Would you stop having faith in God?

Job prayed. He worshiped God. He cried. He was comforted by his friends, and then he argued with his friends. He questioned God. He got angry at God. He demanded an answer.

But one thing Job never did—he never lost faith in God. Though he was sad and angry and upset—even at God!—he never lost his faith.

In the end, God gave Job a new family and restored everything he owned. But we know that couldn't make up for what Job lost. Ever since the beginning, when Adam and Eve disobeyed and goodness was lost, all people have lived in a world of death and darkness. We all lose things, and we don't want a replacement for what we lose—we want all loss and all crying and everything we're afraid of to stop forever. We want everything sad to come untrue. We want the unending life and unlimited love we were created for.

Job was not the One. But another Person was coming who would also lose everything—even more than Job. Not only would this Person lose status, wealth, and family, but He would give up His own life! In the end, His loss would be gain for God's people. The One we're waiting for would be willing to give up everything so that God's people could get back everything they ever lost to death and darkness. His loss and death would bring the unending life and unlimited love all people want.

There is One coming, God promised. He's the One we're waiting for.

Song for family reflection:
"In Christ Alone"

Discuss these questions together

- *What would it be like to have everything and then suddenly lose it all?*
- *How do you think Job held onto his faith? Would you still believe and trust God if you lost everything?*
- *What kind of person would lose everything to save someone else?*

December 19

In the Belly of a Big Fish

From Jonah

Do you know what a *consequence* is?

It's that thing that happens after you do something you're not supposed to do.

For example, you're not supposed to touch an iron when it's plugged in. If you do, you'll burn your hand. Your burned hand is the consequence of your decision.

Sometimes, consequences are small, and sometimes, they are huge. Did you know that there was once a man whose consequence was being swallowed by a gigantic fish?

Jonah was a prophet, meaning that God would tell him what to say, and he would say it. But once, God told Jonah to say something to a group of people that Jonah really didn't like.

Jonah, God said, *I want you to go to the city of Nineveh and give the people this message from Me: They need to repent—turn to Me—or they're going to be in big trouble. But if they repent, I will forgive them*. But Jonah thought they were big meanies, and he didn't want the Ninevites to be forgiven. So he went in the complete opposite direction of Nineveh!

Jonah knew God loved the people Jonah didn't love, and that God would forgive them for their sin and give them unending life and unlimited love. That's why he tried to run away from God and God's instructions.

But you can't run away from Someone who is everywhere. And while Jonah was sailing on a ship away from Nineveh, God sent a huge storm. Jonah knew the storm was his fault, so he took the blame. He went to the other people on the ship and told them, "Throw me overboard! This storm is God punishing me." They were more than happy to do just that, and the storm stopped.

Jonah didn't sink to the bottom. No, he got swallowed alive by a giant fish, whose belly he sat in for three long days (yuck!) On the third day, the fish threw up (yuck again!), and out came Jonah, on the shore, covered in grossness.

God spoke again. *Jonah, I want you to go to the city of Nineveh and give the people this message from Me: They need to repent—turn to Me—or they're going to be in big trouble. But if they repent, I will forgive them.*

This time, Jonah obeyed. And just as he suspected, the Ninevites repented from their sin, turned to God, and were forgiven.

Jonah—like all people—couldn't disobey God without consequences, and he couldn't outrun God either. God always gets His way, and He loves the people we don't like.

Jonah was a messenger who spoke the words of God; the One God's people were waiting for *is* the Word of God.

Jonah spent three days alive in the belly of a fish because of his disobedience; the One God was sending would spend three days dead in a tomb because of His *obedience*.

Jonah took the message of God's love to people he didn't like even though he didn't want to; but there would soon be One who would take the message of God's love to people who didn't like Him because He *did* want to.

Jonah's message led to the forgiveness of many people. Soon, a new message would lead to the forgiveness of more people than anyone could ever count.

There is One coming, God promised.
He's the One we're waiting for.

Song for family reflection:
"Come, Thou Fount of Every Blessing"

Discuss these questions together

- *Why do you think Jonah disobeyed God? Why do you sometimes disobey God?*
- *What were the consequences of Jonah's disobedience? What are the ultimate consequences of disobeying God?*
- *Why do you think Jonah didn't want the Ninevites to know about God's love? Do you know about God's love for you?*

Three Young Men and Their Surprise Guest

From Daniel 3

Remember King Solomon? The really wise man who turned away from his wisdom?

Sadly, King Solomon train-wrecked his kingdom because he stopped listening to God. His poor leadership was only the beginning of bad days for God's people. They disobeyed God *so* much and listened to themselves *so* often and did *so* many bad things to other people, that God finally made them leave the land He had promised them. They were *exiled* (which is a word that means taken away from their home and made to live somewhere else—in this case, a place called Babylon).

God's people must have wondered if they had really blown it for good. Maybe they'd never receive the unending life and unlimited love they were made for.

But there were a few people—even in exile—who trusted in God and hoped in His promises. One was a young man named Daniel, who became a successful advisor to the Babylonian king. Daniel had three friends who also remained faithful to God. Their names were Shadrach, Meshach, and Abednego. And this story is about them.

First, a little background. The king's name was Nebuchadnezzar. (Imagine writing that name on the top of all your papers at school.) Nebuchadnezzar thought he was a pretty big deal. He made all kinds of rules (that went against God's rules) about what people should eat and drink. In fact, he thought he was such a big deal that people should love and worship him rather than God. But Daniel and his three friends stayed faithful to God. They only ate what God said they should, and they only worshiped the one true God.

So what did Nebuchadnezzar do? He had an enormous gold statue built—ninety feet tall and nine feet wide—that represented the greatness of Nebuchadnezzar and his kingdom, and he made a law that everyone had to bow down and worship it. Anyone who didn't obey would be thrown into a furnace of blazing fire.

Shadrach, Meshach, and Abednego knew there was only one God who deserved their worship, so they refused. And of course, that's when their situation got, shall we say, *heated*. The king flew into a rage, threatening to throw them into the furnace. "And who is the God who can rescue you from my power?" he shouted at them.

The three young men knew that God could save them. They also knew He might not. But they were committed to Him no matter what happened. "He can rescue us from the furnace of blazing fire," they said. "But even if He does not . . . we will not serve your gods or worship the gold statue you set up."

The king's anger burned as hot as the furnace, and immediately he gave orders to turn the temperature up even higher. He called on his best soldiers to tie up the three men and toss them in—and in they went.

Now, this is where the story takes a strange turn. Have you ever had a surprise guest show up? Maybe a friend you weren't expecting came over to play? Or you bumped into somebody you knew when you were at the store. Well, King Nebuchadnezzar sat back to enjoy the sight of the three young men being consumed by the fire, when all of a sudden, he sat straight up.

"Excuse me," he said to his advisors, "but we *did* tie up and throw *three* men into the fire, right?"

"Yes, your Majesty," they assured him.

"Then why are there *four* men walking around in there? And how are they untied? And why is that fourth guy shining bright like an angel?"

Immediately, the king called for the men to come out, and out they walked—three of them, unharmed, kept safe by their mystery guest. Shadrach, Meshach, and Abednego were faithful to God, and He delivered them from their fiery trial.

They remind us of the One who is coming, who will walk through a different kind of fire. He, too, will step into the furnace of a king's anger—not the evil anger of a prideful king, but God's good and righteous anger against sin. He won't just walk into the fire with us; He'll walk into it *for* us, so we don't have to.

There is One coming, God promised. He's the One we're waiting for.

Song for family reflection:

"O Come, O Come, Emmanuel"

Discuss these questions together

- *Why do you think Shadrach, Meshach, and Abednego did what was right even when they knew it might cost them their lives?*
- *Why do you think Nebuchadnezzar was so angry about the three men not doing what he wanted?*
- *Who do you think the mystery guest in the fire was?*

The Queen Who Risked Everything

From Esther

Not long after Shadrach, Meshach, and Abednego walked through the fire with their surprise guest, another young Jewish person was in exile. Her name was Esther. Esther was a woman exiled in a country called Persia. Her uncle Mordecai raised her, and he worked in the Persian government. Esther was beautiful.

There was a king in the land whose name was Ahasuerus, and you could argue that he was the most powerful man ever. He was unbelievably wealthy. He ruled over a vast, sprawling kingdom. He could snap his fingers, and more men and women than you could count would rush to his side, ready to do whatever he asked. And, frankly, he acted as you would expect someone with so much power to act—like a big bully.

He was such a bully that one night, when his wife didn't do something he wanted, he had her banished from the palace. Later, when he was feeling sad and lonely, he realized what a horrible mistake he'd made. How would he fill up this loneliness in his heart? Well, some of his servants suggested that he hold a giant, kingdom-wide beauty contest. The most beautiful woman would become the next queen.

Who won the contest? *Esther.*

Esther was brought into the palace and given a comfortable, cushy life, with everything she could ever ask for at her fingertips. She was the new queen, but no one knew she was in the family of Abraham.

Meanwhile, things weren't going so well for Mordecai. He had made an enemy—what you might call a "bad guy," named Haman—who was jealous of Mordecai. And this Haman happened to be the king's right-hand man.

Haman went to the king and told him there was a group of people—God's people, the children of Abraham—who didn't respect the king and didn't obey the Persian laws. Haman said they were no good for the king or his kingdom, and the world would be better off without them. (This, of course, wasn't true. In fact, not long ago, Mordecai had saved the king's life!) But the king listened to Haman. He gave Haman permission to destroy these people—to wipe them all out, completely.

All of God's people in the entire Persian empire would be destroyed. Where was God? Would He help? Would He deliver them? How would His people come into unlimited love and unending life if they were killed in exile?

Just at this moment, Mordecai knew what to do. He went to Queen Esther and told her, "God has put you in the palace for *just this moment*. You can *intercede*," which means something like standing up for someone. "You can speak up for God's people. You can go to the king and save us!"

Esther knew that no one—not even the queen—could waltz into the presence of the king without permission. He could kill her. (After all, he was not very nice to his last queen.) But she also knew Mordecai was right. She mustered up all the courage God gave her and entered the king's presence. She told him about the awful plan, she told him that *she* was one of the people who was going to be wiped out, and she told him that *Haman* was the trickster behind the whole thing.

The king flew into a rage. He turned on Haman, and instead of God's people being wiped out, Haman and all who sided with him were destroyed. God saved His people because of the courage of a young woman who interceded for His people—a young woman whose story points to Someone else.

God would soon send Someone who, like Esther, would intercede for His people—in this case, with the King of all kings. Just like Esther, this One would put His life on the line to save God's people. But He wouldn't only risk His life; He would give His life.

There is One coming, God promised. He's the One we're waiting for.

Song for family reflection:

"Come, Thou Long Expected Jesus"

Discuss these questions together

- *How would you feel if you thought you and all God's people were going to be destroyed?*
- *Would you have had the courage to do what Esther did, even knowing it might cost you dearly? Where do you think she got that courage?*
- *What does it teach you about God that He had already made Esther queen even before the threat to His people?*

Light Shines in the Darkness

From Isaiah

God's people spent a long time in exile. Whole generations were born, lived, and died away from their Promised Land. Many wondered if God had completely abandoned them. Had they missed out *forever* on the unending life and unlimited love God promised to their father Abraham?

During exile, God sent messengers—called prophets—to His people to remind them of His love for them and His commitment to them. Sometimes they came with harsh messages, telling the people they needed to repent of their sin and turn back to God. Other times, they came with gentle messages, telling the people that even though they had completely given up on following God, He would not give up on them.

One of the most important prophets was a man named Isaiah. In one of his messages, he told the people of a "great light" that was coming. Listen to the message God told Isaiah to give the people:

The people walking in darkness
have seen a great light;
a light has dawned
on those living in the land of darkness.

God promised, through Isaiah, that the dark night of exile was going to end, and a great Light was going to shine on them soon.

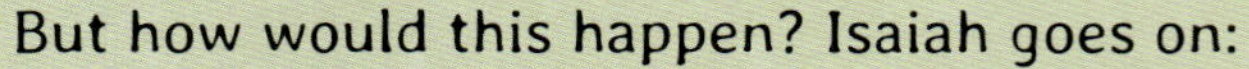

But how would this happen? Isaiah goes on:

For a child will be born for us,
a son will be given to us,
and the government will be on his shoulders.
He will be named
Wonderful Counselor, Mighty God,
Eternal Father, Prince of Peace.
The dominion will be vast,
and its prosperity will never end.
He will reign on the throne of David
and over his kingdom,
to establish and sustain it
with justice and righteousness
    from now on and forever.

Isaiah was making a promise about the One—the One we're waiting for! He told them exactly who to look for: A child would be born who would grow up to lead a kingdom. He would be called "Wonderful Counselor, Mighty God, Eternal Father, Prince of Peace," and He would reign over a vast, prosperous, and never-ending kingdom of justice and righteousness. But not before He suffered.

Like a lamb led to the slaughter
and like a sheep silent before her shearers
he did not open his mouth.
He was taken away because of oppression
and judgment,
and who considered his fate?
For he was cut off from the land of the
living;
he was struck because of my people's
rebellion.

Eventually, the dark night of exile did end, and the people came home. But the promised King was still not there. The people had to keep waiting for Him, but they knew when He came, it would change everything. He would obey God perfectly. He would trust God completely. He would never sin. He would free His people (and all of us) from the exile from God's presence that started when Adam and Eve sinned. And He would do that by suffering Himself.

There is One coming, God promised. He's the One we're waiting for.

Song for family reflection:
"Joyful, Joyful, We Adore Thee"

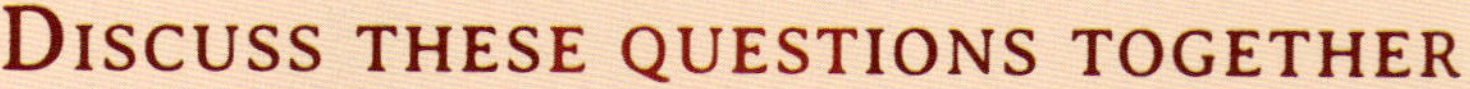

Discuss these questions together

- *Why did God keep sending messengers to His people while they were in exile?*
- *Have you ever had to walk in the dark? What was it like? How does it feel when the lights come on? What do you think Isaiah was trying to say with this idea of darkness and light?*
- *What would it be like to live in a perfect kingdom, with a perfect King, forever and ever?*

The Birth of a Baby Boy

From Luke 1, John 1 & 3

God continued to make promises to His people during the time of Exile, and He eventually brought His people home. But things were never quite the same. The Israelites continued to be mistreated by powerful nations and harsh rulers—like the Greeks and the Romans. And all throughout that time after their return from exile, God stopped talking to them. He was silent.

How would you feel if someone important to you stopped talking to you? Or if you were on the phone with your mom or dad or grandparents, and they just . . . went silent? Would you wonder what happened to them? Would you wonder if they still loved you?

God's people were probably wondering these things about God. When would all His promises be fulfilled? When would the Light shine in the darkness? When would they be given unending life and unlimited love?

The good news is, God did still love them. And He had not gone anywhere. His silence wasn't going to last forever—He was just saving up for the best message yet.

After a few hundred years of God's silence, a man—a priest, actually—named Zechariah, was at work doing his priestly duties. He had the once-in-a-lifetime chance to go into the holy place in the temple to worship God, when all of a sudden, God broke His silence. An angel appeared to Zechariah. He was a messenger sent straight from God. And he spoke.

Zechariah was terrified. And who can blame him? Despite some pictures you may have seen, angels are actually scary-looking!

Now, before you learn what the angel said, you need to know something about Zechariah and his wife Elizabeth. They had never been able to have children, and now, they were old—way too old to have children. Kind of like Hannah, who couldn't have a son, but prayed and prayed until God gave her one. Or maybe even more like Abraham and Sarah, who were also way too old to have kids. Isn't it interesting to read all of these stories about God giving life where it seemed that new life was impossible?

Back to the angel. First, the angel told him not to be afraid. Then he said, "Your prayer has been heard. Your wife Elizabeth will have a son. Your son will turn the hearts of many people to the Lord. And he will go before the Lord to prepare the people for the appearance of the Lord."

Sure enough, Elizabeth became pregnant. When the baby was born, Zechariah and Elizabeth named the child exactly what God told them to name him: John.

Though John was not the One, God created John to prepare the way for the One. Just as the angel told John's father in the temple, John became the greatest messenger God had ever sent to His people. His message could be summed up in two words: "Get ready!"

Get ready for what, you ask? For the Lord. For the Messiah. For the Savior. For the Light that will shine in the darkness. *For the One we've all been waiting for.*

John came to tell people about the Light that would shine in the darkness—the same Light that Isaiah told about. John was not the Light, but he came to tell everybody about the Light and to prepare them for God making all His promises come true by giving His people unending life and unlimited love. There would never again be silence from God because God was coming to be with His people. People wouldn't need to go into a temple to meet with God because God would soon become a human person and live with His people.

There is One coming, God promised. He's the One we're waiting for.

Song for family reflection:

"O Come, All Ye Faithful"

Discuss these questions together

- *What do you think the people thought about God's long silence? Had they lost hope?*
- *Why do you think the same story about miraculous births keeps happening over and over again?*
- *How do you think John felt about his responsibility of preparing the people for the One we're waiting for?*

One More Miraculous Baby

From Luke 1:26–38

In a small, not-so-special town, on an ordinary, not-so-special day, a young girl was minding her own business. Her name was Mary.

Mary, like Zechariah, got a surprise visit: another angel. "You will have a son," he said.

Mary was engaged to be married to a man named Joseph. But she wasn't married yet. And it was impossible for her to have a baby. One hundred percent, totally, completely *impossible*.

Over and over again in the story of His people, God miraculously brought life where there was none. He brought life by creating the world from nothing. He gave life to Abraham and Sarah, to Hannah, and to Zechariah and Elizabeth when they couldn't have children. He saved the lives of Jonah and the three young men in the fiery furnace and all the people through Esther's faithful actions. And He promised unending life and unlimited love to people who didn't deserve it.

All those lives, all those miracles, all those promises, were pointing forward to *this* moment.

"This baby isn't going to be a normal baby," the angel went on. "He's the One you've been waiting for. He will be the Son of God—God Himself, as a human person. You are going to name Him Jesus, because He will save His people from their sins. He is the Son of Adam, the Son of Abraham, and the Son of David. He will be a King forever and ever."

"But how will this be possible?" Mary asked.

"Nothing will be impossible with God," the angel told her.

Finally. This Child, this baby boy, this miraculous birth—the son of Mary is the Son of God and the One who will make all of God's promises come true.

Mary couldn't believe it.

"Go see your cousin Elizabeth," the angel told Mary, "and she'll help you know that it's true."

You see, Mary was cousins with Zechariah's wife Elizabeth. Mary went to see her, and as the two pregnant women saw one another, something remarkable happened: The baby inside of Elizabeth—John, the one preparing the way for the One—started jumping for joy inside of her.

Elizabeth cried out with a loud voice: "You are the most blessed woman, and your Child will be the most blessed Child! You are the mother of my Lord—the mother of the One!"

This was almost too much for Mary, who burst into song. "Praise God!" she sang. "He has done mighty things! He has brought down the high and mighty, and He has raised up the poor and the humble. He has shown us mercy, and He will save us by this Child—*my* Child."

Mary didn't understand, but when she obeyed the angel and saw Elizabeth, she knew it was true. This was the One—the One we've been waiting for.

It all seemed to Mary to be too good to be true. And doesn't it still seem that way? It seems too good to be true that Someone will give us unending life and unlimited love. It seems too good to be true that Someone will crush the serpent, take away our sin, and lead us back into God's presence. It seems too good to be true that Someone will take away death and pain and crying and everything bad and sad.

But you know what the best part is? *It's the truest story that has ever been told.* And all the other stories point to this one.

There is One coming, God promised.
He's the One we're waiting for.

Song for family reflection:

"Silent Night, Holy Night"

Discuss these questions together

- *How do you think Mary must have felt about giving birth to the One we're waiting for?*
- *Does it sound like the story of Jesus is too good to be true?*
- *Do you see how all the other stories pointed forward to this one?*

The Birth of Jesus

From Luke 2:1–7

Finally, the time arrived. Mary was ready to have the baby boy named Jesus.

In those days, Caesar Augustus—who was the king of the Roman Empire, the most powerful nation in the world—made a rule that all the people should be counted (mostly so that the king could feel really special about how big his kingdom was). Because of the census, Mary and Joseph had to travel to a little town called Bethlehem. It was the same little town where King David was born.

While they were there, the time came for Mary to have the baby. But there were so many people in Bethlehem that they could not find any guest rooms. The only place they could find was a stable—a home for animals. And the King of the world, the One we've all been waiting for, the Son of Adam and Son of Abraham and Son of David—the Son of God—was born and placed in a feeding trough for animals.

This was *not* how you would have imagined the birth of this great King. But then again, this isn't a normal King, is it?

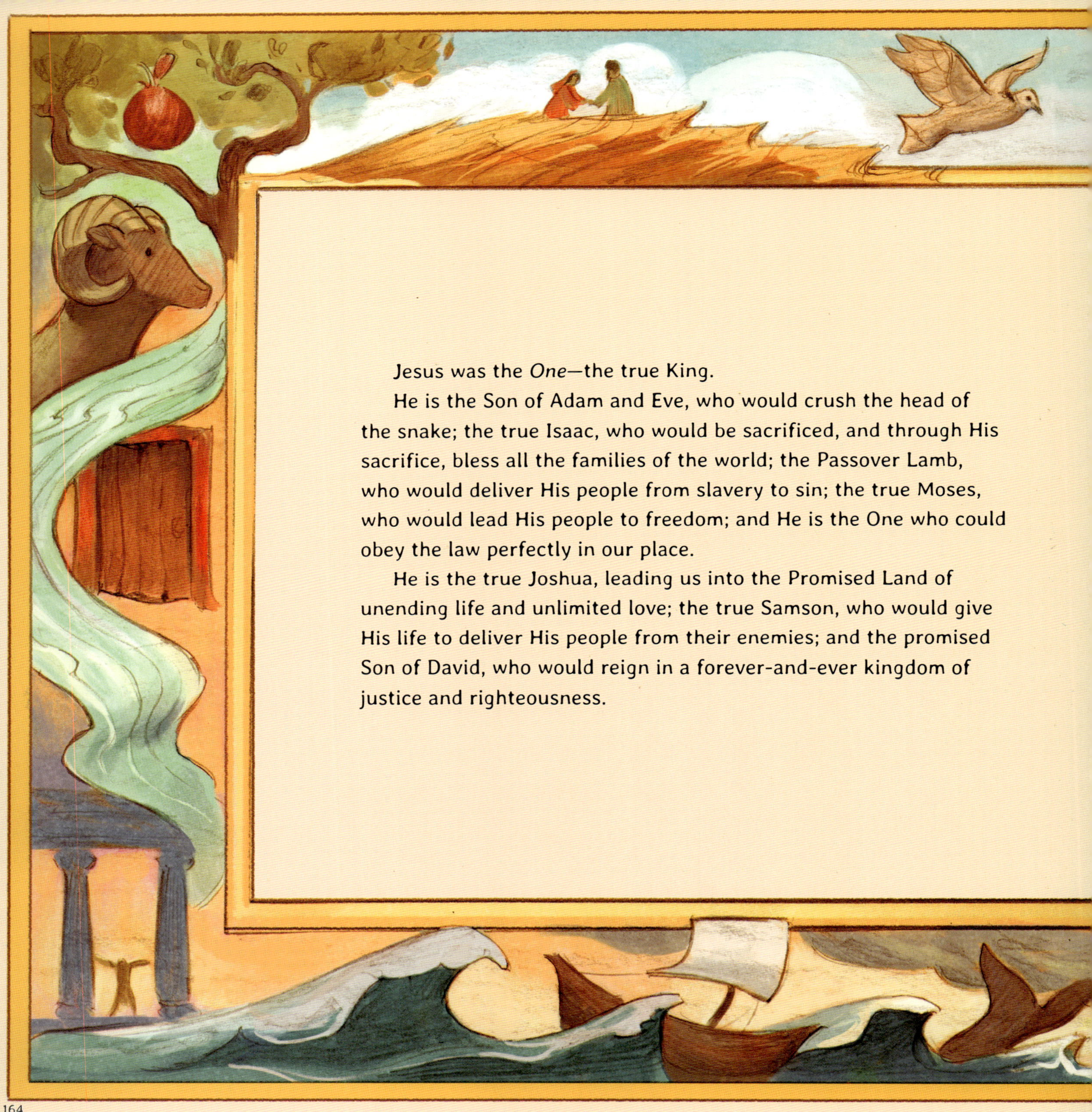

Jesus was the *One*—the true King.

He is the Son of Adam and Eve, who would crush the head of the snake; the true Isaac, who would be sacrificed, and through His sacrifice, bless all the families of the world; the Passover Lamb, who would deliver His people from slavery to sin; the true Moses, who would lead His people to freedom; and He is the One who could obey the law perfectly in our place.

He is the true Joshua, leading us into the Promised Land of unending life and unlimited love; the true Samson, who would give His life to deliver His people from their enemies; and the promised Son of David, who would reign in a forever-and-ever kingdom of justice and righteousness.

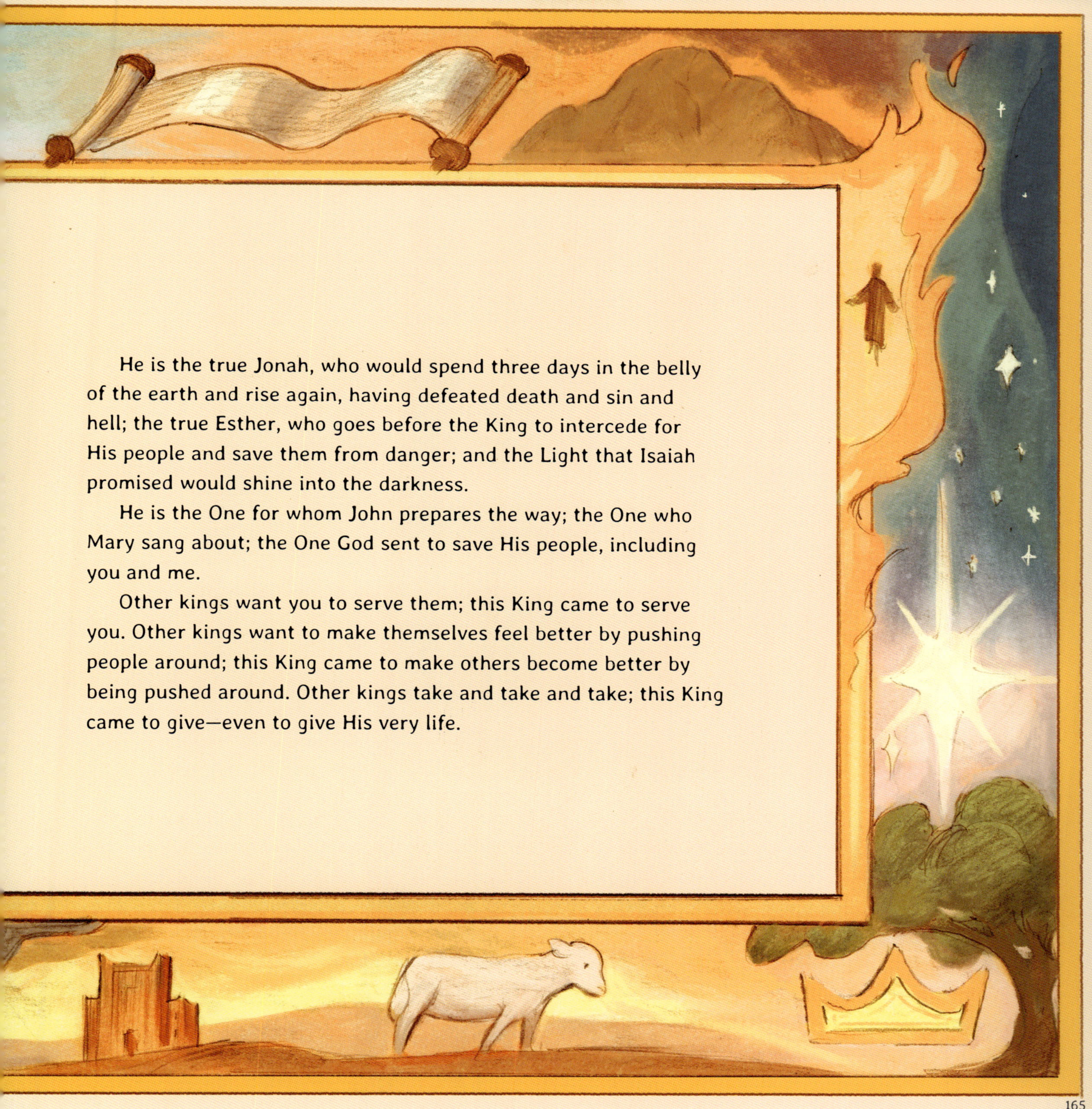

He is the true Jonah, who would spend three days in the belly of the earth and rise again, having defeated death and sin and hell; the true Esther, who goes before the King to intercede for His people and save them from danger; and the Light that Isaiah promised would shine into the darkness.

He is the One for whom John prepares the way; the One who Mary sang about; the One God sent to save His people, including you and me.

Other kings want you to serve them; this King came to serve you. Other kings want to make themselves feel better by pushing people around; this King came to make others become better by being pushed around. Other kings take and take and take; this King came to give—even to give His very life.

You and I—just like Adam and Eve and everyone else to live since them—turn away from God. We are sinful and prideful, and we think we know better than God. We listen to our own hearts, and do what we want to do, instead of listening to God. But turning away from God is turning away from His life and love. We deserve to die because of our sin.

But this Jesus, this King, this One we've been waiting for, He became one of us so that He could live the perfect life we all fail to live, die on a cross to pay the penalty for our sins, and give us the unending life and unlimited love that we were made for.

Other kings expect to be served, but this King was born, lived, died, and rose again to serve people like you and me. Other kings expect to be loved, but this King came to love people like you and me.

He came, as a baby, on that very first Christmas, to give us life that will never, ever end, and love that cannot be measured. And that's the greatest gift we could hope for.

There is One who has come.

He's the one God promised—the One we waited for.

Song for family reflection:

"Hark! The Herald Angels Sing"

Discuss these questions together

- *Why do you think God's Son was born in such a simple way and placed in a manger?*
- *Why did Jesus come to earth?*
- *When Jesus was born, there was no room for Him. Today, you and I can make room for Him in our hearts. What does it mean to make room in our hearts for Jesus?*

About the Creators

Taylor Combs is a pastor in Nashville, Tennessee, where he lives with his wife, Lindsay, and their children. Taylor has a bachelor's degree in Bible and Ministry from Lipscomb University, a Master of Divinity from Southern Seminary, and a PhD from Midwestern Seminary—which is just another way of saying he went to school for a really long time. Taylor loves Christmastime and has very strong opinions about when it's appropriate to start listening to Christmas music (wait until Advent begins!). His favorite Christmas traditions include watching *It's a Wonderful Life* and spinning the Vince Guaraldi Trio's *A Charlie Brown Christmas* on the record player while decorating the Christmas tree.

Aedan and Natalie Peterson are both illustrators based in Nashville, Tennessee. They make a living drawing pictures, which seems sort of silly but is actually very serious, suit-and-tie, "grown-upy" work. It's true, you can find them in their home office Monday–Friday drawing back-to-back in their matching suits and ties. They've each worked for a range of clients including Shining Isle Productions, WaterBrook, Wolfbane Books, We Carry Kevan, and Moody Publishers. When not drawing or painting, they can be found playing with their daughter, Phoebe, who also wears a full suit and tie despite being a toddler.

Acknowledgments

Taylor–

Before the idea of this book was ever presented to me, I worked in book publishing for several years. I know well the truth of the cliché that no book is written alone. Credit is due to the entire team at B&H for making this possible: copyeditors, typesetters, designers, marketers, salespeople (especially Diana: thank you!). Thank you all for the hard work that you put into bringing this book to fruition.

Aedan and Natalie, thank you for the beautiful illustrations on these pages. I truly would not have wanted to make this book with anyone else. Your art is a gift to the church, to the world, and to all who know you (and many who don't!).

A special note of gratitude is due to Lauren Groves. Lauren—a dear friend and fellow member and leader at King's Cross Church—presented this idea to me at a time when I had no intention of writing a book of any kind for the foreseeable future. But when she said I could work with her and our dear friends Aedan and Natalie, it was impossible to say no! Lauren, you worked tirelessly on this project. It exists because of you, and will, I pray, be a gift to many families thanks to your efforts. Thank you, Lauren!

Aedan and Natalie–

We are so thankful to make something like this at all, but to make it with our dear friends is such a huge gift! Thank you, Lauren, for having the vision for this project and letting us be a part of it. Thank you, Taylor, for crafting such beautiful words. And thank you, Diana, for all your work! Your amazing eye and creativity have made the entire book so beautiful and cohesive. What an amazing team to be a part of!

Also, thanks to my (Aedan's) mom, who has watched our sweet daughter more times than we can count while we've worked on these illustrations! Thanks to my (Aedan's) dad for making the best Advent album there is.

Thank you to my (Natalie's) mom, who cherished even my toddler scribbles and my (Natalie's) dad, whose superhero drawings inspired me to be an artist myself.

Sharing Memories

The following pages are for your family to share favorite memories of the Advent season.

Making the Ornaments

These simple ornaments can be made into beautiful keepsakes for your family to hang on your tree for years to come.

You may choose to hang the ornaments on your family Christmas tree, or you can use a Jesse tree—a tree specifically used to prepare for Advent. The name of this tree comes from Isaiah 1:11 which says, "A shoot will come up from the stump of Jesse; his roots, a Branch will bear fruit." Jesse was King David's father, and Jesus is the shoot Isaiah referred to. He is the Messiah all people looked forward to, so a Jesse tree is a physical representation of Jesus's coming. This can be a real tree, a felt or cloth hanging, or whatever you'd like it to be.

Use the ornaments found on the following pages or, if you need more, go to this book's website to download a copy of the ornaments.

Simple cut-out ornament

For those in need of a simpler method, cut the ornaments out, poke a hole in the top, and tie a string through it. Just be sure to store them in such a way that they won't get bent from year to year.

Felt ornament

If you'd like the ornaments to go with a felt tree, consider using felt cloth as the backing for each ornament. Simply cut out felt circles three inches in diameter, cut out each ornament, and use tacky glue to attach the ornament to the center of the felt circle. If you're sticking the ornament to a felt tree, that's all you need to do! If you'd like the ornament to hang, be sure to leave some space at the top to cut or punch out a small hole and add some string so you can hang each ornament on your tree.

Wooden ornament

To make a sturdy wood ornament, purchase natural wood slice ornaments at least three inches in diameter. Make sure that the ornaments you purchase already have holes cut in the top to add a hanging string. To attach the ornaments, apply a very thin layer of tacky glue to the wood and then place your cut-out ornament over the top. Make sure the glue is thin so that the ink doesn't run. Also, be sure that the ornament is secured at all edges so that the edges don't come back up year after year. Give your ornament plenty of time to dry, and then hang them on your tree each day of December.

Tip: You can use this same method with round, flat acrylic ornaments.

Bulb ornament

Finally, you can always add these ornaments to classic bulbs. Simply purchase clear, fillable ornament bulbs that are at least three inches in diameter. Cut out the ornaments, and then place them in the bulb. You may choose to secure them with hot glue or just let them lie in the bulb for a more organic look. Consider adding shredded basket grass to the back of the bulb to fill the space a little more. You can also tie a ribbon around the top of the ornament to make it look even more ornate.